# *Writing American History*

## ESSAYS ON MODERN

## SCHOLARSHIP

**HIGHAM, John. Writing American history; essays on modern scholarship. Indiana, 1970. 241p 70-108209. 6.95. SBN 253-19700-7**

Higham (Michigan) is widely respected both for his books (e.g. *History*, CHOICE, June 1965) and seminal articles on the present condition of historical writing in America. For this volume he has collected and updated several of his most important pieces, together with others less well known. Writing beautifully and incisively, Higham outlines the growth of American historiography, analyzes some of its methodological and philosophical problems, and suggests ways of overcoming confining limitations. He urges historians to move beyond the so-called consensus approach and be more evaluative; he points the way toward more cooperation between the social sciences and history; he explores the alternate approaches to intellectual history. Higham even offers an essay example of the kind of history he advocates. Anyone and everyone concerned with American history should read this book. There is no comparable work, either in subject matter or intellectual sophistication. Absolutely essential for every college library. Extensive notes and index.

CHOICE        JAN. '71

History, Geography & Travel

North America

E
175
H 63 w

# JOHN HIGHAM

# *Writing American History*

## ESSAYS ON MODERN

## SCHOLARSHIP

*Indiana University Press*

BLOOMINGTON / LONDON

Copyright © 1970 by Indiana University Press

Published in Canada by Fitzhenry & Whiteside Limited, Don Mills, Ontario

Library of Congress catalog card number: 70–108209

ISBN: 253–19700–7

Manufactured in the United States of America

*To Merle Curti*

# CONTENTS

*vii*

# *P R E F A C E*

W<small>HEN</small> M<small>ICHAEL</small> A<small>RONSON</small> <small>OF THE</small> I<small>NDIANA</small> U<small>NIVERSITY</small> P<small>RESS</small> suggested the desirability of gathering my essays on American historiography into a book, the proposal seemed temptingly simple. Though vaguely aware of some dead or decaying passages in those essays, I was sure they could be excised in a week or two of work. The last thing I wanted to do was to reconsider a vein of writing that had always in my mind been secondary to my research interests, and sometimes an extended diversion. Now, several months later, I look back with dismay and astonishment at the reconsideration that forced itself upon me.

The essential character and point of view of these commentaries on American historiography remain largely unaltered. But I have endeavored to bring all of them up to date, and I have clarified and amplified many passages that were excessively compressed. One essay, which has been widely reprinted, was so embarrassing to reread in the light of subsequent scholarship and my own present understanding of the issues, that I have replaced it instead of revising it. Chapter 3 is therefore an entirely new appraisal of American intellectual historians. The last chapter in the present volume also appears in print for the first time.

Altogether, the essays collected here give a selective account of the writing of American history in the twentieth century and of its cultural context. Although this book may be read independently, it is in effect a supplement to my earlier book, *History* (1965), which was written with the collaboration of Leonard Krieger and Felix Gilbert as a volume in the Princeton Studies of Humanistic Scholarship in America. That book offered a compact synthesis of the whole sweep of modern historiography in the United States. This book is more informal, more evaluative, and deals in greater depth or in special ways with aspects I know more about,

In addition to a unity of subject, these essays are also linked by my involvement in certain perennial antitheses of intellectual life. One has to do with the contrast between scientific and humanistic styles of thinking. Another, which is political and social as well as philosophical, grows out of the rival claims of diversity and unity, or of conflict and consensus. I have always discovered myself between these poles, responsive to both while reacting against the exclusive claims of either. Consequently I have found the same axes helpful in defining the problems and possibilities of American culture.

The habit of taking positions in the center, somewhere between dialectical extremes, can be enervating. But I do not think it need be. Particularly in the study of history, the truth seems most commonly to lie on a middle ground. The trick, of course, is to know *what* middle ground, between *which* extremes, and so to locate not a mere intermediate zone but a center of gravity, where one can stand and prepare to move forward.

*Ann Arbor, Michigan*                                          J. H.
*July, 1969*

# *Writing American History*

## ESSAYS ON MODERN SCHOLARSHIP

# PART I

---

*Rival Methodologies*

# 1

---

# THE SCHISM IN
# AMERICAN SCHOLARSHIP

SHORTLY AFTER PUBLISHING *my volume in the Princeton Studies on Humanistic Scholarship in America, I was asked by the director of the project, Richard Schlatter, to give a paper about the series and about the general state of the humanities in America. I thought I might piece together, from my own book on history and from the other volumes in the project, an overall sketch of the development of the humanities in modern America. I discovered, as the historian always does when he broadens the frame of reference, that new questions arose. They could not be answered from our preceding studies of individual "disciplines." The very concept of the humanities had been shaped by a context—and was thus part of a history—extending well beyond the limits of our specialized volumes.*

*The first version of this paper was given at a conference in Princeton on November 6, 1965. In improving the paper, I had the inestimable benefit of criticism and comments from colleagues at the Center for Advanced Study in the Behavioral Sciences, which also gave me the time to do this research and writing. Originally printed in the* American Historical Review, *LXXII (October, 1966), 1–21, the paper is reprinted here with some reorganization in the interest of greater clarity.*

*I*

IN THE EARLY 1960's, when Pablo Casals played at the White House and Robert Frost helped to inaugurate a President, a few university professors and administrators resolved to gain federal funds for "the humanities." Each year the National Science Foundation, which had been created in 1950, was pouring greater sums into the hands of scientists engaged in "basic research." Many other national agencies subsidized studies deemed to have some practical relevance to national defense, health, or social welfare. With President Kennedy's blessing, plans were being drawn for a proposed National Arts Foundation to encourage the creation, display, and performance of art. Surely, in the midst of so much affluence, such hunger for excellence, so much concern about the quality of American culture, the humanities need not remain unassisted. The scholars who study such matters as literature, philosophy, and history wanted recognition too.

Early in 1963 the American Council of Learned Societies launched an organized campaign. Along with certain other scholarly bodies, it created a commission to report on the state of the humanities and to point the way to national aid. President Barnaby C. Keeney of Brown University became chairman. Keeney and his associates never succeeded in winning the attention of President Kennedy. But before long they made a crucial decision that gained powerful allies: they decided to emphasize the inseparability of humanistic scholarship and the creative arts.[1]

For this approach the Commission on the Humanities had some justification in principle. One of the tasks of the disciplines it represented was to discourse about art, and academic endeavor would certainly be greatly enlivened by closer relations with the cultural world outside the universities. Keeney, as he told Congress, wanted the humanities and the arts to fertilize one another.[2] At the same time he must have realized that the problems of a ballet dancer differ from those of a professor of ancient history at least as much as his problems differ from those of a physicist. Beneath all affirmations of the reciprocity of art and intellect lay a bond of expediency: the humanities would have a better chance of gaining federal aid if their drive were tied to the more broadly based and fully developed campaign for governmental support of the arts.[3] The commission put aside all thought of asking for an enlargement of the National Science Foundation to include the humanities. It rejected also the possibility of assigning the job to the U.S. Department of Health, Education, and Welfare. Instead, it came out boldly in 1964 for a National Humanities Foundation that would take responsibility for both the humanities and the arts.[4]

A plan for a National Arts Foundation, which August Heckscher had devised as special consultant to President Kennedy, had passed the Senate in December 1963. Its sponsors did not take kindly at first to this intrusion from the scholarly world. But after the arts bill failed to pass the House and a few congressmen became interested in a similar plan for the humanities, the desirability of joining forces became apparent. Characteristically, President Lyndon B. Johnson put his weight behind a new bill that would incorporate within one National Foundation on the Arts and the Humanities two independently functioning endowments, one for the arts, the other for the humanities.[5] This measure, authorizing each endowment to make annual grants of as much as ten million dollars, was enacted in September 1965. Just a year earlier the backers of the commission's original humanities bill had requested a much more modest appropriation while anticipating a legislative campaign of several years for that. But Congress was mesmerized by the soaring prestige of culture, which had now been authoritatively proclaimed a mission of the Great Society. The administration bill won assent with an ease and rapidity that seemed almost miraculous.[6]

During the congressional hearings and debates, academic spokesmen were usually wary of specifying what they meant by humanities. The alliance with the art establishment, nevertheless, seems to have encouraged an emphasis on moral and aesthetic "enrichment." The humanities, according to their  proponents, have to do with qualitative judgment, with a "broad" culture, with an intangible "excellence." Keeney at one point described the humanist as a person who studies human activities through methods other than quantitative.[7] Underlying the whole discussion was an assumption of the nonscientific character of the humanities; they are subjects distinct from and competitive with the sciences.

The belief that knowledge and the students thereof are divisible into two bodies, one scientific, the other "humanistic," is indeed one of the constitutive ideas that frame contemporary intellectual life. The new institutional arrangements for subsidizing scholarship reflect that dualism. They may also reinforce it, since the new foundation seemed to detach the humanities from the sciences and associate them with the dissemination of art. The result was a division of labor between two federal agencies that give away money for academic research. The National Science Foundation, austerely excluding anything that might be controversial, supports the social sciences insofar as they "can be studied by objective methods, which will yield independently verifiable results."[8] The National Endowment for the Humanities embraces other subjects—literature, linguistics, history, philosophy, archaeology, jurisprudence, the study of art and music—and "those aspects of the social sciences which have humanistic content and employ humanistic methods."[9]

While federal policy produced these separate institutions for nourishing the "two cultures," some leading thinkers were coming to believe that the cleavage between them is the very condition the contemporary intellect most needs to overcome. C. P. Snow's famous address in 1959 on the breakdown of communication between men educated as humanists and men educated as scientists seems to have dramatized in America as well as Great Britain a renewed search for continuities.[10] Not all integrationists adopt the same strategy, of course. Some, who are highly monistic, would impose a single logical structure on every kind of knowledge. Others, more pluralistic, see a mixture and gradation of diverse components running through the range of intellectual disciplines.[11] Yet both deny that a sharp or absolute dichotomy between two types of inquiry should exist. In the study of man today, the development of "area studies" and the growing influence of such intellectual hybrids as psycholinguistics and the history of science are demonstrating the practical irrelevance—indeed, the actual hindrance—of a dualistic scheme to what many of our best scholars are doing. Is it possible that the "humanists" have at last achieved official recognition in America at the very moment when the antagonistic confrontation of the two cultures is beginning to yield to new unities and diversities?

If so, we can assist the reorganization by appreciating how fluid and indistinct the line between these cultures has actually been. In the study of man it is by no means easy to say what is science and what is "merely" humanistic. To some extent distinctions between the scientific and the humanistic are useful and important. The terms do suggest differences in method, in aim, even in habit of mind. As a recent study of English schoolboys shows, there may be quite extensive differences in personality and life-style between students who specialize in the physical sciences and those who are drawn to the study of literature, art, and history.[12] Yet the patterns overlap and interpenetrate so much, particularly in the study of man, that a distinction between "humanities" and "social sciences" misleads and stultifies. In other words, the contrast between humanistic and scientific methods, significant though it is, does not logically require a similar division in subject-matter. The effort to align method with subject, which induces us to dignify academic departments by calling them "disciplines," has created a false cleavage between two coalitions of "disciplines," both of which strive for internal solidarity. For the most part, self-conscious efforts to be "interdisciplinary" have aimed at convergence within one coalition or the other, thus widening the gulf between them and actually restricting the circulation and development of those who find themselves on either side of the divide. The destruction of those privileged sanctuaries we have labeled "humanities" and "social sciences" might open up a more fruitful rivalry and interplay between scientific and humanistic methods.

## II

When we speak of science in the relatively restricted way that is current in the United States, we commonly mean the systematization of knowledge under general laws that can be verified and amended by further observation. Thus scientific thinking seeks analytic generality. It abstracts what is measurable from finite things in the interest of formulating precise and entirely unambiguous concepts about them. Such procedures are applied, however, as they seem useful, in different degrees to different kinds of data and questions. They do not belong solely to the social studies, nor do they preempt those studies.

The methods that are often called humanistic also have a legitimate place, and should have an important one, in all branches of scholarship. Yet we have no single humanistic strategy. Perhaps the most that can be said is that humanistic approaches predominate in all efforts to preserve and appreciate the complexity of experience. These efforts include the use of expressive rather than technically precise language, a greater interest in individual events than in general laws, a reliance on qualitative rather than quantitative judgment, and a subjective grasp of a totality in preference to a dissection of its parts. Most, if not all, scholarship needs some proportion of humanistic and some proportion of scientific thinking. Why then have the students of man in American universities become segregated into rival camps, one labeled "humanities," the other labeled "social science"? The polarization is surprisingly recent and distinctively American.

Consider, for example, how scholarly activity is organized in western European countries. Although American influence has counted heavily in recent years, the American distinction between humanities and social sciences has not yet become a major organizing principle in higher education. In British universities the great divide is between the faculty of arts and the faculty of science. Social studies belong to the faculty of arts, which feels profoundly separated from the faculty of science, particularly in the large universities.[13] The

French pattern also resists differentiation between social and humanistic studies. The arts faculty, in France usually designated the
faculty of letters and human sciences, includes most of the social disciplines, but economics and politics quite illogically come under
another jurisdiction, that of the powerful faculty of law.[14] While
arrangements vary from one country to another, nowhere do we find
the tripartite division into humanities, social sciences, and natural
sciences that characterizes the American college.

Similarly, the general agencies that sponsor original inquiry in
Britain and France have not, on the whole, distinguished sharply
between two ways of studying man. The British Academy was
founded to promote "the moral and political sciences, including
history, philosophy, law, politics and economics, archaeology and
philology," and it still conceives of itself as capable of speaking for
the whole world of learning outside of the natural sciences. In addition to this private body, which receives from the crown a modest
subsidy for miscellaneous research purposes, Britain has created an
array of official research councils and cultural agencies over which
presides a single Secretary of State for Education and Science.[15] In
France a still more centralized public body, the Centre National
de la Recherche Scientifique, is charged with the development of
learned research of all kinds. It has two general subdivisions, one
for *les sciences exactes,* the other for *les sciences humaines.* The latter
groups together thirteen "sections" dealing with culture and society.
These "human sciences" are anthropology, classics, economics,
geography, history, linguistics, literature, Oriental languages and civ-
ilizations, politics and law, sociology, psychology, and philosophy.[16]

It is true that the social sciences in some countries, perhaps largely
as a result of American influence, have been developing in recent
years a corporate identity. In France this appears in certain research
institutes, notably the Sixth Section (Sciences économiques et
sociales) of the Ecole Pratique des Hautes Etudes. In Britain the
government established a Social Science Research Council in 1965
under the chairmanship of Michael Young.[17] The notion of
"science" as applied in Europe to human affairs, nevertheless,
retains a certain indefiniteness. It may mean, as the term *Wissen-*

*schaft* does in German, any organized body of knowledge cultivated for its own sake; whereas "science" to Americans usually
suggests something necessarily rigorous and restrictive. In Europe
the social sciences have not come under the wing of the natural
sciences, as some did in the United States through the National
Science Foundation. Nor have European literary and historical
scholars forged a competing organization to sustain nonscientific
studies. In a rough way it might be said that Europeans distinguish
principally between natural science and the study of man, whereas
Americans are more likely to draw a sharp boundary between
"science" of every sort and "the humanities," Evidently Americans
have designed for themselves a somewhat distinctive map of
the geography of high culture, on which social sciences and humanities appear as rival confederations disputing territory they jointly
occupy.

This does not mean, of course, that European maps necessarily
make better guides for intellectual activity. Europeans tell us, for
example, that the relatively strong position in the United States of
a body of social sciences, situated intermediately between the
natural sciences and the cultural studies, tends to reduce the distance
between the two. Surely there is a certain justice in this observation,
in spite of the inclination of some American social scientists to
identify themselves exclusively with natural science and the contrary impulse among humanists to disavow both. The European
comparison may not yield a superior model, but it enables us to ask
why the United States is not truly enjoying the continuity between
science and humanism that its eclectic institutions would seem to
facilitate.

The question may be sharpened, and answered in part, by some
historical perspective. The present cleavage between the humanities
and the social sciences in the United States has materialized only in
the twentieth century. The very categories of contemporary dispute
—the whole vexed issue of defining the humanities and social
sciences—played little part in American academic life before the
First World War.

In the nineteenth century the great jurisdictional conflict in higher education separated the defenders of a traditional classical curriculum from the champions of the natural sciences. The social sciences did not enter into the dispute, since they emerged as separate and distinct subjects only toward the end of the century. It was the warfare between classicist and natural scientist that produced the modern conception of humanistic studies. But the head-on clash occurred in England rather than the United States. In this country intellectual categories remained much less clear.

In the nineteenth century "humanism" or "the humanities" meant primarily an education in the literature and culture of Greece and Rome. That kind of education functioned in England to sustain an aristocratic social order. The leading English schools and universities doggedly enforced the Greek and Latin classics as the main substance of education because those ancient, nonutilitarian subjects supplied the cachet of a gentleman. Against all this, Herbert Spencer and Thomas Huxley spoke for a modern scientific education, and they spoke in tones charged with the grievances of the utility-minded middle classes.[18]

The controversy forced a gradual widening of the concept of "the humanities" beyond its primary reference to classical studies. To Matthew Arnold and others like him—wise and flexible defenders of a gentlemanly education—the term "humanities" acquired a secondary, extended meaning that included the whole range of secular subjects treating human experience and culture. Arnold saw that the traditional educational ideal could be saved from the scientific onslaught only by freeing it from narrow class interests and classical molds. Accepting a fundamental dualism, he argued that education should enable "a man to know himself and the world." To know the world, that is, "non-human forces," he should study nature through science. To know himself, that is, "the operation of human force, of human freedom and activity," he should study the humanities. Both are important, but human-centered knowledge should predominate, for it is ethical, social, and aesthetic as well as intellectual.[19] This distinction helped to preserve in Britain the ascendancy of a literary culture. It defined as humanities all subjects that concern man as distinct from physical nature.

Thus it kept the social studies under humanistic auspices and somewhat constricted their development.

Although Arnold's influence was widely felt in America, conditions here did not allow so confident or extensive a definition of the humanities to prevail. In fact, American educators in the nineteenth century seldom talked about "the humanities." Until after the First World War one finds only sporadic and usually casual references. A writer in 1910 commented on "the sharp line of demarcation between the sciences and the 'humanities' so noticeable at the present time."[20] His examples were English, however, and his object was to reconcile underlying educational philosophies. It is true that American educators, like their English contemporaries, debated the importance of the classics throughout most of the nineteenth century. It is also true that the underlying ideological conflict, expressed in England through opposition between the humanities and the sciences, divided the faculties of American colleges and universities as well. Should higher education be predominantly literary and ethical or chiefly specialized and scientific? On one side were men who valued personal distinction as the great end of education and feared the growth of scientific materialism. On the other were those who championed research as the glory of the modern university.[21] What was lacking in America was not a clash of values but a sharp polarization of "disciplines."

The differences reflected the more eclectic character of American higher education. The keen edge of class envy did not aggravate disputes over academic reform. Being less exclusive, American colleges more readily diluted the classical program with modern studies, both scientific and literary. Americans, in defining the aims of a liberal education, were characteristically more willing than Englishmen to acknowledge the value of the sciences. By eschewing the humanistic label, American proponents of "liberal culture" kept clear of its parochial associations.[22]

In the early twentieth century reference to "the humanities" cropped up more frequently in American educational discussions, often in a sense significantly narrower than Arnold's but also broader than the usage of the English classicists. Whereas Arnold expanded the humanities to embrace the whole realm of man as distinct from physical nature, President A. Lawrence Lowell of Harvard and President William Rainey Harper of the University of Chicago spoke of "those subjects which represent the culture of the past." Science explains the existing world; the humanities preserve our heritage from earlier times.[23] This definition rested partly on the great prestige history acquired in nineteenth century thought. Literature, philosophy, and indeed most of the subjects treating human affairs at the turn of the century were taught historically. The study of history in various forms had superseded the study of the classics as the chief vehicle for enabling man to know himself. Yet the definition of the humanities as historical exposed a weakness in their American status,

The dangerous feature of the historical approach was its strongly conservative bent. It was too commonly out of touch with the main forces in American life, too much engrossed with continuity and tradition in a land of flux and improvisation. The academic humanists tended to divorce the past from the present. In the early twentieth century the study of literature hardly reached Alfred Tennyson or Robert Browning, the study of philosophy went little beyond G. W. F. Hegel, and the study of history and politics dwelt on the origins of deep-rooted institutions.[24]

As the ideal type of humanistic scholar of the early twentieth century, one thinks of Professor Godfrey St. Peter, so lovingly portrayed in Willa Cather's novel, *The Professor's House* (New York, 1925). Author of an eight-volume *Spanish Adventurers in North America,* St. Peter is an unworldly man of fine scruple, detached from the pushing, materialistic life around him. His family has induced him to build a shiny new house, but he cannot bear to leave the dowdy old one in which his great work was written. The new house is utilitarian; it threatens to cut him off totally from a richer, more humane past. Thus the dilapidated house with its cluttered, dingy study is a symbol of discontinuity between the humanities and modernity. In addition, the professor had a brilliant student who constituted for him a living link between the present and past. He was a potential successor, not vocationally—for Tom Outland had actually become an inventor—but in a deeper sense. The young man perpetuated and renewed a culture that included both science and art, both tradition and innovation. But this legatee of the professor's integrity and wholeness had died in the World War; an upstart now exploited his work. Past and present had split apart in the professor's world and could not be joined again. The professor himself had become an anachronism. Written in the 1920's, the novel was more than a portrait; it was an elegy.[25]

## *III*

Willa Cather's imaginative representation of a certain type of humanistic professor, immobilized and defeated by his isolation from contemporary life, coincided with the full development in American consciousness of a contrasting image of the social scientist. The social scientist stepped forward as a truly vital figure, relatively indifferent to history but wholly committed to the problems and needs of the present time. This idea began to influence American academic culture about the turn of the century. It evolved simultaneously with the reputation of the humanities as tradition-bound disciplines.

When the newer social studies emerged into academic respectability toward the end of the nineteenth century, their position in the university was happily vague. They sprang from diverse antecedents: partly from philosophy, partly from history, partly from an inductive spirit. The new disciplines had much to do with speculation on the one hand and with empiricism on the other. Although concerned with the contemporary world, they were imbued with evolutionist theories and engaged in explaining the historical process.

Similarly, the concept of social science was ambiguous and indefinite. The term "social science" had originated in France in the late eighteenth century. It meant the application to society of laws similar to those of the natural sciences; it was used by men who wanted to be scientist-statesmen, planning a new social order.[26] In the course of the nineteenth century, however, the positivist and the reformist implications of the term tended to drift apart. Some thought of social science as a quest for basic laws. For others it was practical knowledge of community problems: how to cope with epidemics, illiteracy, crime, and the like.[27] The social sciences were as indistinct as the humanities.

Thus Edmund J. James, one of the early entrepreneurs of American social science, was making a modest bid for definition and recognition in 1890 when he founded the American Academy of Political and Social Science. James had charge of the new Wharton School of Finance and Economy at the University of Pennsylvania. He was one of the first to conceive of politics, economics, and sociology as an interrelated set of disciplines distinct from other sets. In a presidential address to the Academy in 1897, he argued for a tripartite structure within universities, giving the social sciences a status equal "to the old historical subjects of university instruction, history, grammar, and philosophy on the one hand, and to the newer subjects grouped under the head of the natural sciences on the other." The claim did not rest on any explicit theory. It was frankly expediential. "If we organize the political and social sciences in such a way that they can be set over as a group of social sciences against a group of natural sciences," James advised, "we may be very certain that they will be more adequately cared for."[28]

James conceded that intellectual developments within the various fields might bring about a different alignment. The organization of scholarship was in such flux that no one could foretell what the future classification of the sciences might be. In spite of a rapid growth of social studies in the early years of the twentieth century, they still exhibited little sense of collective identity. Each of them was asserting its own individuality, while all shared with the older disciplines a common style of scholarship.[29] In contrast to James's expediential separatism, some hoped that the new subjects would bring more continuity between the literary and the scientific aspects of education. Commenting in 1902 on the emergence of "a new body of studies," John Dewey saw them as agencies for healing divisions between past and present, between science and culture:

While the struggle between the classicists and the scientists has been going on, a new body of studies has been gradually making its way, and is now reaching the point of conscious insistence upon its own claims. History, sociology, political science, and political economy may certainly claim to stand for the humanities. Quite as much as any linguistic phenomena, they represent fundamental values of human life. Yet they are the offspring of the scientific method.[30]

Just after World War I, while these categories were still fluid, an opportunity arose for institutionalizing a broad, eclectic spirit in the study of man. Ten American learned societies—including the philosophers, the Orientalists, the economists, the historians, and the sociologists—resolved in September 1919 to create a central body to be called the American Council of Learned Societies Devoted to Humanistic Studies. The initiative came from abroad. An International Union of Academies was forming in Paris. Conceived in European terms as a federation of all *les sciences humaines,* it would embrace "the philological, archaeological, historical, moral, political and social sciences." The Americans needed a national organization of that sort in order to be properly represented. It would also promote research and liaison among the constituent disciplines, in imitation of what the National Research Council was beginning to do for the natural sciences. Two historians took the lead in founding the ACLS. Charles Homer Haskins, Harvard's famous medievalist, and Waldo G. Leland, secretary of the American Historical Association, organized the preliminary meeting. Leland wrote the constitution.[31] They were acting out the ascendancy history still enjoyed in the study of man.

One might have expected in 1919 that a sense of common interests among the "learned societies devoted to humanistic studies" would evolve into a general intellectual partnership. Instead the reverse occurred. In spite of (and even in a way because of) growing uneasiness over the fragmentation of scholarship, the humanities and the social sciences parted company, and each group defined itself as exclusive of the other. Premonitions of the schism had appeared among historians in the years just before the war, as they began to quarrel over the extent to which they should ally themselves with social scientists, a dispute reflecting a new awareness that the social sciences were no longer clearly allied to them.[32] In the general

academic community the split proceeded so rapidly that a survey of
*Research in the Humanistic and Social Sciences,* published in 1928,
began with an apology for its divided title:

The term "humanity" ought to suffice; properly understood, it of course
embraces the social sciences equally with linguistics, literature, and
archaeology. The rapid development of economics, political science, and
kindred disciplines in the past twenty years has, however, led to a habit,
at least among social scientists, of limiting "humanities" to the older
"cultural" studies.[33]

Soon the habit became too deeply ingrained for apology. Instead,
there developed in the 1930's and after an affirmation and institu-
tionalization of distinctive roles. Reorganization of the Rockefeller
Foundation in 1928 resulted in a Division of Humanities and a
separate Division of Social Sciences. During the following decade
many colleges and universities followed suit. Frequently they added
humanities courses, programs, and comprehensive examinations.[34]
In 1945 Harvard's enormously influential report, *General Education
in a Free Society,* cast its recommendations in the framework of a
threefold division between natural sciences, social sciences, and
humanities. According to the Harvard committee, the separation
was justified by academic tradition (how rapidly innovation becomes tradition in the United States!) and by a difference in the type
of thinking characteristic of each area.[35]

The initiative behind the schism came mostly from social
scientists. During the 1920's political science, economics, sociology,
and related fields entered a phase of ambitious growth. Their
younger leaders forged a common identity exclusive of the students
of literature, art, philosophy, and most historians, and that produced
a defensive, self-conscious reaction within the older disciplines. The
chief act of secession was the formation in 1923 of the Social Science
Research Council. Several of the learned societies already represented
in the ACLS constituted the new council. Though most of them
remained titular members of the ACLS, the SSRC was much better
financed and more tightly knit, and for all save the historians it
quickly became far more consequential. The historians who were

trying to breathe life into the ACLS pleaded with Charles Merriam, the founder of the Social Science Research Council, not to disrupt a united effort of "the whole group of the humanistic sciences." But Merriam had a program that would render the very idea of "humanistic sciences" obsolete.[36]

At the core of the social science movement of the 1920's was a new ideal of organized, collaborative research. In the projects of the SSRC, the Brookings Institution, and similar agencies, the watchword was interdisciplinary cooperation, *but only between social scientists*. Through teamwork, interdisciplinary conferences, and the like, scholars solidified an image of themselves as social scientists and gave their loyalty to the dream of an integrated science of man. Within a decade of the founding of the SSRC the first approximation of the dream was appearing: a monumental *Encyclopedia of the Social Sciences*. The opening sentence of its preface sounded the theme of the whole movement: "It is only in comparatively recent years that the interdependence of the social sciences has come to be recognized as a concept necessary to their progress."[37]

It was not just organization that cut social scientists off from humanistic scholars; it was also aim. Such men as Merriam, John B. Watson, the behavioristic psychologist, Paul Lazarsfeld, the pioneer of public opinion surveys, and Karl Llewellyn, the legal realist wanted to create a pure science of behavior.[38] That science would have to rid itself of any taint of the European, "humanistic" propensity toward speculative thought or normative judgment. It would have to eliminate values from the actual process of inquiry, though they might properly guide the initial selection of problems and the utilization of conclusions.[39] Certainly not everyone who called himself a social scientist coveted neutrality, precision, and quantified abstraction to the same degree. In each discipline "soft" approaches coexisted with "hard" ones. Among anthropologists, particularly, the poetry and passion of human experience remained vividly alive, and most of the major figures in American sociology—in contrast to the rank and file—retained important humanistic components.[40] The primary goal for more and more social scientists was, nevertheless, rigor, the compelling task, a refinement of methodology. This trend, emerging strongly during the interwar period, reached a crest in the 1950's.

A puristic spirit, narrowing social science to a study of what man is, took hardly more account of what he had been than of what he ought to be. The new social science movement not only excluded the normative, it tended to expel the historical from the center of interest. In part, this present-mindedness was a concomitant of the methodological quest for rigor. Contemporary data, collected under controlled conditions, readily amenable to statistical manipulation, were orderly, precise, and thus more attractive than the helter-skelter materials left by the past. In part, also, historical consciousness suffered from a passionate interest in theory construction, which accompanied the mathematization of problems. In manipulating abstract relationships and in creating systems, the social theorist usually wanted to disembarrass himself of the concreteness and particularity of history as far as possible.

In a larger sense many social scientists doubtless shared in the indifference, if not outright hostility, of the modern temper toward the past itself. Discarding an evolutionary framework for the study of society, they immersed themselves in the phenomena of immediate experience partly because they were coming to doubt the relevance of historical continuities to a world transformed. They were caught up during the twenties, thirties, and forties in a wide-reaching desire for emancipation from tradition, precedent, and outmoded forms. Against the dry, aloof historicism prevalent in several disciplines, against for example the ACLS's neglect of the contemporary and preoccupation with such tools of historical scholarship as a paleographical guide to Latin manuscripts,[41] against a past detached from the present, the would-be scientists flung themselves into a present sundered from the past. In England, France, and elsewhere, social scientists never broke so sharply from history and thus never achieved so distinctive an identity.[42]

Meanwhile in America the rising prestige, the brash self-confidence, and the strong corporate spirit of the new type of social scientist threw traditional scholars on the defensive. Among some, a tendency—which had lingered in the classical tradition of education—to disparage science as "merely" instrumental was greatly sharpened. Irving Babbitt and Paul Elmer More won a considerable following in the 1920's for their "New Humanism," an intensely antiscientific polemic against modern culture. They championed an education based on the wisdom of the past in order to check the disruptive effects of scientific and social experiment.[43] Other scholars turned in the opposite direction, seeking to reform their respective disciplines sufficiently to qualify as scientists themselves. Under the leadership of I. A. Richards, some literary scholars began to apply systematically the principles of psychology to the experience of literature. In philosophy John Dewey's program, designed to put all judgments on an experimental basis, prepared the way for the emergence in the 1930's of a stricter logical positivism. Among historians a vigorous minority tried to convert themselves and their colleagues into full-fledged, up-to-date social scientists.[44] In each of these disciplines, and in linguistics as well, the reformers abandoned or at least foreshortened the historical matrix of earlier scholarship. Perhaps never before had the cleavages within each discipline become so pronounced.

By the 1930's a third response to the confusion and the loss of initiative materialized. A campaign developed to redefine the humanities in a way that would stress their positive moral relevance to contemporary life. As early as 1933 we find Leland, president of the ACLS, accepting the division between social sciences and humanities, and taking satisfaction that the formation of the SSRC enabled the ACLS to devote itself entirely to the humanities, since they deal with "the manifestations of man's spiritual existence."[45] Two years later the Rockefeller Foundation launched a new program to "bring the values of the humanities more directly into contact with daily living" in the hope of contributing to "a spiritual renaissance." In 1940 a doctoral candidate at Teachers College, Columbia University, published a monograph on "the sudden dramatic revival" of a term that now denoted "a field comparable in breadth to the Social Sciences and the Natural Sciences. . . ." "On every hand today," the editor's foreward stated, "—in the press, the radio, the school—we are called upon to defend 'the Humanities'

. . . ."[46] In the 1940's a torrent of books and articles with such titles as *The Meaning of the Humanities,* "The Future of the Humanities," "The Humanities Begin to Fight," *The Rebirth of Liberal Education,* or *Education at the Crossroads* poured from the presses. The stream has persisted sufficiently to convince an amused English observer, Professor David Daiches, that a strenuous defense of the humanities goes on all the time in America.[47]

These apologetics differ from more sporadic references to the humanities in the early twentieth century not only in volume but in emphasis. No longer did a "rich heritage" seem the chief gift of the humanities. Above all, they are said to offer a "liberating" knowledge of choice, preference, and taste. "The element common to the humanities," the apologists have agreed, "is their common concern with values."[48] Consequently such words as "spiritual," "moral," "humanizing," "human dignity," "valuation," "design for living," and "broad vision" recur continually.

In the last three or four decades many professors have endeavored to live up to the claim by enlarging their evaluative skills. Under the tyranny of fact that ruled the study of history and literature in the late nineteenth and early twentieth centuries, scholars took values for granted. Characteristically, they assumed that investigation of circumstances and events would of itself lead to conclusions about merit. Since then an increasing number of academic humanists have embraced the act of evaluation as their major task. To some leading historians, interpretive judgment conditioned by present needs has become a legitimate—indeed a preeminent—function. In the study of literature the New Criticism and a fresh social criticism broke the dominion of literary history.[49] Avid interest in criticism, particularly of modern, living writers, led in turn to assimilation of novelists and poets, then artists and musicians—men whose whole business is the projection of values—as regular members of university faculties.

Yet the claim of a special status for the humanities as value-laden disciplines was excessive, even transparent. For one thing, there has never been the slightest agreement about the proper role of values in any field. In spite of all efforts to practice what the apologists were preaching, a great legion of scholars in every discipline still shrank from making explicit, deliberate judgments about merit. Some supposedly humanistic fields, notably philosophy, actually became in the 1940's more antiseptic—more skeptically critical of all value judgments—than ever before, and in every field an ideal of objective neutrality has remained strong.

For another thing, value statements should occupy just as important a place in the social sciences as they have in the humanities. Many American educators have grown accustomed to talking as if qualitative appraisal and choice reside more properly in the study of language than in the study of politics, as if they belong more suitably to the criticism of music than to the criticism of society. Partly as a result of this disjunction, American academic life produces, along with a vast amount of aesthetic judgment, a paucity of expert social and moral judgment.

The rise of so misleading a conception of the humanities may be explained in considerable measure as a defensive strategy to protect and comfort those who felt left behind by the emergence of an organized social science group. But the kind of defense and its timing also suggest deep uneasiness about the state of values at a particular juncture in American history. The impassioned defense of the humanities as the repository of values broke out in the 1920's and sharply intensified in the 1940's; it clearly reflected the moral and intellectual turmoil two world wars unleashed.

In the aftermath of the atomic apocalypse, it is easy to forget how deeply the First World War shook the confidence of sensitive people in the stability and humaneness of their civilization. The submarine and poison gas, especially, gave a shocking demonstration of how science could be put to immoral ends if its advances were not somehow matched by a deliberate cultivation of values.[50] Thus, when the threat of totalitarianism aroused American intellectuals to a great need for moral rearmament in the 1930's and 1940's, it built upon an already awakened sense of imbalance between power and principle in modern life. Appeals for revitalizing the humanities typically associated the increasing threat of political tyranny and brutality with a mechanized, scientific efficiency. The humanistic scholar would have to defend "human values against war abroad and against socio-economic and scientific-naturalistic fatalism at home."[51] The desire for spiritual guidance from the humanities clearly reflected these interlocking concerns.

## IV

Now times have changed. America has certainly not outlived the anxieties of the period from 1917 to the early 1950's, but our perception of the continuing crisis of our time has greatly altered. Though fears of an impending breakdown of civilization persist, they are no longer so clearly focused. Few today can trust the redemptive power of any one segment of knowledge. The dream of producing an integrated, immaculate social science has given way to more modest, carefully delimited expectations, which permit the quantification of knowledge to proceed more widely and soundly than before; and the compensatory vision of the humanities as the organized conscience of Academia has correspondingly dimmed. At a time when the whole professoriate—humanists as well as scientists—has become privileged, affluent, and deeply uncertain of itself, the question of its moral center is posed in an altogether new way.[52] Thus the conditions that produced the great schism in American scholarship have substantially changed.

How much the schism itself is healing remains uncertain. In some ways it is less pronounced than it was a decade ago. On the institutional side the Rockefeller Foundation has merged its Humanities and Social Sciences Divisions. The ACLS, after undergoing two reorganizations between 1946 and 1956, no longer adopts a superior attitude toward the modern or the mundane. It collaborates easily and effectively with the SSRC on a whole range of matters. Evidently some "disciplines" are also becoming more hospitable to methodological diversity. Analytic philosophy, some authorities report, is overcoming the excessive rigor of a few years ago.[53] Meanwhile, an increasing number of historians are learning to think in more systematic, problem-oriented terms; and in the social sciences an interest in processes of modernization and economic growth has brought theory back into conjunction with historical data on a very considerable scale. It is now fashionable to deplore rivalry between the three cultures. Yet the institutions, nomenclature, and habits of mind produced by their cleavage persist. No one has yet found an organized strategy for hastening their demise.

To sum up: The humanities as we know them today in America comprise no meaningful or coherent entity. To conceive of them still as distinct from the social sciences in the exercise of qualitative judgment is to perpetuate stereotypes colored by the dislocations of a generation ago. The current definition of a humanist arose chiefly as a reaction against the self-conscious exclusiveness of a new breed of social scientist. It was an effort to establish a countervailing identity. The identity was always artificial; it has become an encumbrance.

We know by now that no group of disciplines has a monopoly on values or on measurement. The intellectual commerce we need perhaps most today spans the divide we have created between humanities and social sciences. Our existing categories tend to deprive some disciplines, notably history, of analytic abstraction; they discourage others, such as social psychology, from acquiring historical complexity. As a result of the great schism, by and large, we still assign much too low a priority to evaluative finesse in the social sciences and to criteria for measurement in the humanities. Consequently, we have too little "art" in one camp, too little "science" in the other, and not enough breadth of mind in either.

Will the National Endowment for the Humanities widen the breach in American scholarship? At first it seemed likely to do so, but its policies have shown an attractive flexibility. In 1968, for example, additional legislation authorized the Endowment to support the "application of the humanities to the human environment," and a new emphasis was thereupon put on projects dealing with current national problems.[54] Still, the Endowment's budget remains meager, its need for congressional approbation keen. It would be pleasant if some deus ex machina—some great foundation or endowment— would supply the initiative for an overhauling of priorities and relationships in the study of man. In all likelihood, however, the academic world will have to reconstitute itself.

# PART II

---

*Polarities in*

*Intellectual History*

# 2

---

# INTELLECTUAL HISTORY

# AND ITS NEIGHBORS

About 1940, as an undergraduate *at The Johns Hopkins University, I came, unwittingly, under the simultaneous influence of two different types of intellectual history. One proceeded from Professor Arthur O. Lovejoy, who had only recently retired and whose influence on the campus was still powerful. What a thrill it was to hear him give a scintillating paper that year at the annual meeting of the American Historical Association! Yet the historians under whom I studied were teaching quite a different sort of intellectual history. The difference became clearer when I arrived in graduate school and found that my new mentor, Merle Curti, had forged an approach to intellectual history that was explicitly and diametrically opposed to Lovejoy's.*

*The present paper explores the underlying implications of the divided heritage I had received. This divergence in approaches to intellectual history may be understood as occurring under the influence of the broader cultural cleavage discussed in the preceding chapter.*

*In recent years the contrast between external and internal types of intellectual history has lost much of its sharpness in the practice of American scholars, just as the schism between humanities and social sciences has lessened. Nevertheless, the issue is a perennial one. The present essay is therefore reprinted substantially as it first appeared in the*

27

Journal of the History of Ideas *(XV [June, 1954], 339–47; used with the permission of the* Journal*). I have softened the last paragraph and added a major reservation in an addendum (see pages 38–40).*

Surely no genre of scholarship in recent years has exceeded intellectual history in the variety of academic subjects from which it draws practitioners. Philosophers, literary scholars, historians, theologians, political theorists—these and other heterogeneous types have converged upon one another, bringing very different interests, backgrounds, and methods to a more or less common task for which none was initially trained. It is, then, an unavoidably interdisciplinary enterprise on which they have entered, and intellectual history exhibits the marks of any such enterprise in our day: effervescence and confusion. Along with an exhilarating sense of pioneering and the pleasure of breaking through conventional walls have come some problems of direction-finding. Perplexities abound when one stops to ask: What am I doing?

The answers given to that question in an interdisciplinary context will depend partly on one's "foreign policy," the attitude adopted toward other disciplines encountered on the same terrain. In scholarship as in diplomacy, one may be an expansionist, or an isolationist, or an internationalist. The expansionist point of view, extending over new ground the claims of the academic homeland, may breed a good deal of jostling and rivalry as representatives of established fields claim competing spheres of influence over intellectual history. Isolationists may venture abroad without realizing that they have done so, and pursue their separate ways through the tumult while steadfastly ignoring it. Proponents of collective security may inspire one another and borrow from one another, sometimes to the extent of entering into formally cooperative arrangements like the American Studies programs that have developed in many colleges and universities since the 1940's. For these intellectual history provides the point of convergence and thus the central area of study.

Since we live in an age of internationalism, the dangers of

academic isolation or expansion are evident enough. Those of cooperation should not get out of sight. In trying to fuse insights and procedures derived from unlike fields, intellectual historians may lose a sense of direction; they may exchange customary means of analysis for formulas of the lowest common denominator, which answer all questions and clarify none. At the risk of imposing my own kind of imperialism on intellectual history I begin with the simple proposition that it is a branch of history. Whatever else it involves, it deserves from students of every academic persuasion a central allegiance to the aims and methods of historical study. I propose, at any rate, to appraise the dimensions of intellectual history and its relations to other subjects from the vantage point of its historical foundations.

I assume that history characteristically reports particular and unique human experiences in an attempt to elucidate their connections through time. Above all the historian wants to know why a sequence of happenings took place as it did. To find out, he links those specific experiences one to the other with the aid of appropriate generalizations. He does not, like the scientist, move away from particulars toward a system of general, verifiable concepts; nor does he, like the artist, move into particulars to disclose the values inherent in them. The historian moves *between* particular experiences to learn how one begot another. But to establish these relationships he employs both the values of the artist and the inclusive propositions of the scientist; in his hands tested constructs and untestable values become functional to a narrative task.

Basically intellectual history differs from other varieties because it has a distinctive subject-matter. It concentrates on experiences occurring inside men's heads. It centers on man's inner experiences, the experiences he has in thinking. Many academic disciplines, of course, share an interest in man as a thinking being, but they concern themselves either with one kind of thinking or with thinking in general. Intellectual history is unlimited in scope, but it should respect the historian's method. It deals with all sorts of thoughts but deals with them discretely, in terms of their genetic relations in time and place.

The historian's concern with ideas in all their specific variety compels a close and precise attention to the documents that reveal them; and this practical condition in turn has often encouraged misunderstanding of the permissible range of intellectual history. Partly because the most discriminating and readily available documents are produced by highly articulate people, intellectual historians have tended to write mostly about the thoughts which circulate among intellectuals. Meanwhile a substantial, perhaps a preponderant part of the academic world relegated to social history the study of the moods and beliefs of the man in the street, reserving for intellectual history the study of high-level ideas.[1] To define the field in this limited sense is to miss much of its complexity and significance. At least by construing it narrowly we run the risk of pre-judging its affiliations and character. Intellectual history may (though it need not in any single instance) embrace simple attitudes in simple or complicated people as well as systematic knowledge and speculation. It includes Little Orphan Annie as well as Adam Smith. I am not of course proposing our absorption in men's trivial reactions to the passing scene. History is selective; it looks for the bolder contours on the landscape of the past. In examining the mental landscape the intellectual historian selects the relatively enduring ideas, which sway a considerable number of people over a period of some time; but he may select them from the comics as well as from the philosophers.

Whether he deals in popular myths or in metaphysics, the intellectual historian must perform the historian's task of relating the particular inner happenings that interest him to a context of other happenings that may explain them. Here a quest for definition grows more difficult. What kind of other happenings? What type of context? Where should the connective generalizations serviceable to intellectual history lead? These questions have given rise to two rather distinct answers, which amount almost to two different conceptions of the discipline. In one view the connections lead outward to an external context of events and behavior. Intellectual history becomes an investigation of the connections between thought and deed. Crane Brinton expressed a version of this approach in emphasizing as intellectual history's primary task the uncovering of relations between what a few men write or say and what many men actually do.[2] On the other hand a second school has insisted principally on establishing the internal relationships between what some men write or say and what other men write or say. This kind of intellectual history directs attention away from the context of events in order to enlarge and systematize the context of ideas. It seeks the connections between thought and thought.

The distinction between an internal and an external history of thinking is, I believe, widely appreciated, although the proponents of each have seldom ventured into explicit controversy beyond an appeal for emphasis.[3] Having had little debate, we have only begun to assess the respective ramifications and consequences of each approach. Yet such assessment must precede an adequate understanding of the nature of intellectual history and its place in the spectrum of knowledge, for the two approaches contain their own underlying assumptions, lead to different affiliations, and suggest contrasting objectives.

Hardly anyone today would argue the total wrong-headedness of either the internal or the external view of intellectual history. Indeed many scholars seem increasingly concerned with combining the two. The difficulties involved in any real merging of them, however, are far more than technical. At bottom each approach expresses a fundamental philosophical commitment. Often accepted implicitly, one commitment or the other directs scholarship more than scholars realize. They may refuse a categorical choice; they may work under the tensions of a divided allegiance. But they can hardly serve two masters with equal loyalty. The issue lies between two ways of conceiving the human mind; and entangled in each is a divergent view of human nature.

A primary interest in the outward links between thought and deed presupposes the notion that mind at its best or most characteristic is functional. Mind makes its mark by serving the practical needs of the workaday world. The relationship between thinking and the concrete circumstances of life acquire importance in the light of the functionalist's respect for the utility of the mind as an instrument of survival. At the same time a functional orientation supplies a rough yardstick for measuring the historical significance of ideas. The test is action, and the importance of an idea approximates that of the deeds associated with it. By this criterion, for example, a persuasive propagandist like Tom Paine might loom larger in history than a frustrated genius like Henry Adams.

On the other hand the internal approach to intellectual history rests upon quite different assumptions. A concern with the inner affinities among and the structures within ideas neglects functional criteria. Instead, the historian assumes that mind at its best or most characteristic reaches beyond practical needs to create values and achievements that have their own excuse for being. The mind pursues objectives somehow "higher" (or at least more noteworthy) than survival, and in place of the yardstick of action one must apply some internal standard to measure its most significant output. The logical consistency of a sequence of thought, the elaboration of a world view, the achievement of a reverberating insight, or the power of an idea to bear further intellectual fruit—these become the norms of an intellectual history pledged to the sheer creative vitality of the human mind.

Parenthetically it is worth noting that the theories of the intellectual process at issue here point toward still larger alternatives. A view of the mind calls forth a view of human nature. If the mind creates in ways that are neither bound by nor referable to the demands of an external environment—if ideas have a life of their own—then human nature bursts and transcends the patterns of the natural world around it. If, on the other hand, mind interests us as an agent of bio-social adaptation, we tend to assimilate human nature to an encompassing system of nature.

Without venturing to cope with the whole problem of the nature of man, it is easy to see objections to either conception of the mind as a controlling principle in historiography. Functional presuppositions are chargeable with devaluing mind. By reducing thought to a series of responses to situations, the functionalist treats it as merely auxiliary to the main business of life. He tends to neglect what his standards cannot appraise—the inner "go," the spontaneity, or the qualitative richness of mental phenomena. He can tell us little about the persistence of an intellectual heritage after the environment has grown hostile to it; still less can he account for the quite impractical ways in which the mind seems to pour forth religious and artistic symbols.[4]

The dualistic assumptions behind the internal history of thought create contrary difficulties. These assumptions tend to divorce thinking from doing and to confine it within categories that have no reference to the world of material circumstance. A separation from events forces an increased degree of subjectivity on intellectual history, since all the elements in the story are then intangibles. With the aid of publishers' records we can trace the circulation of books, but we can never with the same precision trace the circulation of ideas. We can observe the meeting of two armies and feel that the destiny of an idea hangs upon their encounter, but we can never quite so clearly see the meeting of two ideas. Furthermore the notion that mind has its own distinctive and superior goals involves an intellectualistic bias. Ideas capable of the most subtle or systematic articulation become the center of attention and are endowed with special potency. Intellectual history narrows to the history of intellectuals, and, among the products of thought, literature and philosophy assume a privileged status. Carried far enough, the same bias leads to a sweeping assertion of the primacy of ideas in history, just as a functionalist bias ultimately debases ideas into passive echoes of events.

If no student of ideas can escape some preference for one or the other of these two positions, surely all can profit from the fullest understanding of the possibilities as well as the limitations inherent in each. For such understanding the professional historian has a strategic location. His academic territory lies between the humanities and the social sciences. Now the subjectivism of the internal approach appears most typically and completely in humanistic scholarship, while the functionalism of the external view is characteristic of the social sciences. The distinction certainly is not sharp nor is the correspondence exact, for too many cross-currents have blown between them to permit the humanities or social sciences to follow entirely separate ways. Literary scholars like Vernon L. Parrington, deriving stimulus from social scientists, have weighted intellectual history with a functional emphasis, while an occasional writer on the other side of the fence—like the psychoanalyst Erich Fromm—has made fruitful use of humanistic insights.[5] Still, in their main thrust the humanities and social sciences have diverged.[6] The former have inclined toward the qualitive exploration of an inner world of values and imagination. The latter, seeking quantitative measurements of human phenomena, tend to objectify ideas and values into forms of behavior. And the internal study of intellectual history has developed particularly within the value-oriented humanities, just as the external history of thinking has benefited especially from the behavioral emphasis of the social sciences. Perhaps historians—without final allegiance to either domain—can see further into the opportunities of intellectual history by learning from the example of each.

Among the many branches of history, intellectual history lies especially close to the humanities and has received from them its chief support. (On the other hand, economic history with its wealth of measurable data has felt the impact of the social sciences more than any other branch, while having the least contact with the humanities.) Certainly the humanities have influenced the writing of intellectual history far more directly than have the social sciences. Perhaps the most central contribution has come from philosophy, which is the critic of abstractions. In its role as one of the humanities, philosophy seeks to harmonize and clarify the most basic and general propositions involved in value judgments. It is hard to see how an internal analysis of thought can proceed without some philosophical training. From it we receive skill in definition, in discriminating meanings, in detecting assumptions, in formulating issues. These abilities come into constant play in intellectual history because the factual units with which it principally deals are not events we can observe directly but rather ideas and sentiments, which we must define in order to know. An internal history of the connections between ideas obviously calls for especially close philosophical scrutiny. A few philosophers such as Arthur O. Lovejoy have made important advances in the writing of intellectual history by demonstrating ways of grasping the underlying unities that run through many diverse provinces of thought. Other philosophers have worked in the history of philosophy, which differs from intellectual history by interesting itself primarily in the clarification and cogency of doctrines and only secondarily in their genetic relationships. By and large the philosophers' overriding interest in abstractions has kept them from contributing as much in substance as in method. Few philosophical scholars do justice to history's density, its richness of context. It is significant that a philosopher's proposal to trace the history of liberal social thought in modern America should turn out to be a brilliant analytical critique of five men, seen in terms of a single unifying theme.[7]

Literary scholars have more than made up for the aloofness of most philosophers. Intellectual history, written chiefly from an internal point of view, has become a leading concern in departments of literature. Relying heavily on philosophy and history, these scholars have resurrected many of the movements of thought which have supported and pervaded literary achievements. The distinctive contribution which the best students of literature make is not, I think, the analytical precision characteristic of the best philosophical inquiry. Rather it is a sense of the imaginative and emotional overtones in the history of thought. The literary scholar should have an ear sensitive to the resonance of ideas. If he has, he can communicate the passions and aspirations woven through them. He can add an internal dimension to intellectual history by capturing the fusion of thought and feeling. His studies, however, often leave historians unsatisfied by adapting intellectual history to the purposes of literary criticism. One who feels a primary obligation to sharpen aesthetic judgments will naturally employ intellectual history as a means of vivifying literary documents instead of using all documents as means of understanding why men thought and felt the way they did.

The humanities, then, tend to celebrate the finer products of mind, and in doing so they bring to a focus all of the characteristic consequences of an internal approach; a sensitivity to qualitative distinctions, an exaltation of creative thought, an appreciation of subjective criteria for judging it, a restricted sphere of interest and a limited body of materials. How different the prevailing temper in the social sciences! There an attempt to describe the uniformities in human affairs encourages an ideal of quantitative measurement. There the subjective categories appropriate to value judgments are rejected for principles derived from observations of how men behave.[8] There a respect for the molding force of social controls replaces the humanistic emphasis on creative thinkers. There scholars struggle with massive data to interpret the life of the mass of mankind. Insofar as he studies ideas, therefore, the social scientist is most likely to want to learn how numbers of people put them to work within a larger pattern of living. His stress on quantity, objectivity, and behavior will lead to external analysis.

Few social scientists these days take much interest in the past, and few have contributed directly to intellectual history, though we cannot ignore such notable exceptions as Tawney and Weber. The ideals of social science have, however, gradually filtered into the historical profession and there have exerted a somewhat roundabout influence on intellectual studies. Although each of the social disciplines deserves separate appraisal, I want simply to mention three general ways in which we can profit from more direct contact with them.

First, the social sciences may yet teach us something about how to count. Certainly statistical analyses are much more difficult with historical than with contemporary data, and the difficulty increases the further into the past one goes. Even with voluminous records we can probably never count ideas but only certain outward tokens of intellectual life. But any advance toward mathematical precision should clearly seem desirable to those who value exact knowledge. Who knows, for example, what new light a statistical historian might cast on changing attitudes by counting the appearance of certain "loaded" words or phrases in nineteenth century magazines?

Quantification works better for large aggregations than for small ones, and the social scientist typically deals with large ones—with crowds and classes and age groups and cultures. We need to study his procedures if we are going to fulfill the whole range of intellectual history. The internal analysis of the humanist has applied chiefly to the intellectual elite; it has not reached very far into the broad field of popular thought. The blunter, external approach of the social sciences may lead us closer to the collective loyalties and aspirations of the bulk of humanity.

Finally the social sciences offer a multitude of tentative generalizations and classifications, which can enrich our interpretative schemes if we use them cautiously. Very likely few principles of human affairs are exactly applicable outside of the historical epoch that conceived them. But we bring our notions and hunches to the past in any case, so we may well find, in social sciences, hypotheses that discipline the historical imagination. These fields can guide us especially in formulating generalizations that connect thought and behavior; for the social sciences—in contrast to the humanities— have lavished attention on functional problems.

So far I have tried to show how two types of intellectual history, each shaped by a characteristic assumption about the mind, get aid and stimulus from the two realms of knowledge in which those assumptions find a natural locus. But this is not an end to the matter. For all of its interdisciplinary affiliations, intellectual history, like any historical enterprise, must move toward its own goals. Here the internal-external dichotomy presents a final face. In my view intellectual history confronts within the field of history two different tasks, each related to one of the two approaches in question. On the one hand, intellectual history needs to develop a viable degree of autonomy as a branch of history. It needs a more coherent form and structure of its own in order to escape subordination to other disciplines and a subordinate place among the fields of history. This self-fulfillment should come largely through clarification of the inner connections between ideas. It depends, therefore, principally on internal analysis.

Intellectual history has a second task exactly the reverse of autonomy: a task of synthesis. The history of thought must contribute what it can to the organization and understanding of history as a whole. In some sense all human activity has a mental component, and intellectual history is displaying increasing usefulness as an integrative tool. This synthetic objective is approachable by studying the linkage of ideas with political, social, and economic events. It depends ultimately on external analysis.

Now that my argument is complete I fear that I have made too much of it. In the practice of historians the line of cleavage is never absolute. Most historians take some account of both perspectives and of both objectives. Their work gains subtlety through a skillful blend, just as the two types of intellectual history advance through mutual interaction. The difference, then, is one of emphasis.

Indeed, the very nature of history as a field of study militates against an exclusive choice between theoretical alternatives. Historians can be quite arbitrary about restricting the range or the nature of their investigations if the restrictions promise a sharpening of focus. Such restrictions, however, have only an expediential and tentative status for the historian, because his distinctive commitment as a scholar is to grasp the existential wholeness of the particular experience his interest has fixed upon. Whereas other disciplines try to serve some nonhistorical or trans-historical canon of intelligibility, history respects the multidimensional complexity of the human record. Its students tend to cultivate an eclectic spirit; they distrust sharp boundaries either in method or in subject matter. In the work of the best historians formal differences between one kind of history and another become especially blurred. We need to examine such differences, not to widen the breach but rather to seek better ways of combining their disparate possibilities.

\* \* \*

In the sixteen years that have passed since this paper was written, very little progress has been made in applying the technique of content analysis to problems in intellectual history, in spite of the tremendous possibilities for this kind of research that have opened in the meantime through the development of the computer. Three exceptions relating to American history, none of them written by professional historians, are: Richard L. Merritt, *Symbols of American Community, 1735–1775* (New Haven, 1966); Louis Schneider and Sanford M. Dornbusch, *Popular Religion: Inspirational Books in America* (Chicago, 1958); and Richard de Charms and Gerald H. Moeller, "Values Expressed in American Children's Readers: 1800–1950," *Journal of Abnormal and Social Psychology*, LXIV (1962), 136–42, a study undertaken in conjunction with David C. McClelland's much broader attempt to quantify historical trends, *The Achieving Society* (Princeton, N.J., 1961). These are interesting, worthwhile ventures, but I now feel less sanguine than I once did about the contribution such work can make.

The chief difficulty is one of formulating problems that cannot be managed better by traditional styles of historical research. In order to secure reliable findings, the content analyst must construct in advance of detailed research a system of categories for classifying the verbal symbols he proposes to count. Once the system is defined and the research is begun, the units of content to be classified and the categories into which they are separated must not vary. Whatever does not fit those categories must be left aside. Inevitably, this process drastically simplifies the information in the sources under scrutiny; for the more systematic one's methods become the smaller is the proportion or the range of data one can study relative to the universe those data are supposed to represent.

Problems of sampling, reliability, and validity are always formidable in this kind of research, and they become almost insuperable in tracing standardized verbal symbols over any considerable span of time: the meanings the symbols convey are subject to many unpredictable changes, which the very design of research tends to screen out. In contrast to the rigid procedures essential to content analysis, traditional historical research goes forward with a maximum of flexibility. The historian reads his way into a cluster of experience by permitting one source to lead him to another he had not known about and by allowing his increasing familiarity with that time and place to alter progressively his categories and even to transform his whole conception of the problem. In historical inquiry every step toward the systematization of research, involving as it does the exclusion of data the system is not designed to handle, enhances the risk of insensitivity. Historians seeking greater methodological rigor must ask themselves how far they can go in restricting their inputs without a net loss in the results they may attain. In intellectual history the evidence to date suggests considerable caution.

Meanwhile in the study of popular culture much headway has been made in recent years through standard techniques of historical and literary analysis.

# 3

## THE STUDY OF AMERICAN

## INTELLECTUAL HISTORY

ALTHOUGH THE TENSION *between external and internal approaches will doubtless persist indefinitely, it no longer seems to many intellectual historians as crucial as it was. Too much insistence upon it may have the effect of trapping students in a dichotomy that no longer dominates and inspires the best work in the field. I have therefore written this essay to give a wider view of intellectual history. I have sought to bring out the variety of objectives it has served in different ways at different times; and I have taken special note of another polarity, the importance of which we are only now rediscovering, though it too is deeply rooted in the practice of intellectual historians.*

*Twenty years ago, as a new-fledged Ph.D. just beginning to teach, I had the privilege of giving a paper bearing the present title at the First Congress of Historians of Mexico and the United States. It was a cautious paper, an early effort to size up the kind of history I had chosen to teach and hoped to write. It was published in the* American Historical Review *in April, 1951. In 1960, at the invitation of Charles A. Barker, I gave a more pointed paper on the same subject at a Conference on the Historical Study of American Culture. That paper, which was published in the* American Quarterly, *XIII (Summer, 1961), 219–33, raised some of the themes of the present essay; but we were still overwhelmingly preoccupied then with the opposition between external and internal analysis. The present essay was written at no one's invitation and for no purpose but to do fuller justice to the task I brashly attempted twenty years ago.*

## I

To DEFINE INTELLECTUAL HISTORY by deducing its scope and aims from the methods it employs, as I have done in the preceding essay, is to make only a schematic model for the subject, an abstract and static framework. If we would understand the forms in which intellectual history has actually manifested itself in America, we shall have to look beyond the logic of the discipline (if indeed it has one) to consult its history. The same could be said, of course, for any body of knowledge. None of them reveals itself fully until it is understood historically; for knowledge has no predetermined organization but grows and changes in the flux of human purpose and experience. Intellectual history, however, must be rated as more indeterminate than many other "fields," such as military or constitutional history. Unlike these, intellectual history does not single out one segment of behavior for special attention. It deals, potentially, with every sort of thought and emotion. And since all human actions express a thought or a feeling, intellectual history has no province that is peculiarly its own. It lurks in every historical document; it informs every historical event. We speak of intellectual history only when states of mind emerge into the foreground of interest, only when the subjective level of experience becomes the primary focus of the historian's curiosity. Why that should happen at particular times and in particular ways is perhaps the most interesting question that can be asked of the study of intellectual history.

Historians, obviously, do not give much attention to the influence of thought and feeling unless they rate it as important. But they may also neglect the history of thought if they take its importance for granted. An activity forces itself to the center of a historian's vision only if it poses problems for him. It must seem to him a realm of significant change, an area rich in potentialities yet full of difficulties, a field strewn with impediments as well as excitations. In the eighteenth and nineteenth centuries a few pioneers wrote the first major works that may be called intellectual histories. These men, as we shall see, had special reasons for considering ideas and intellectual achievement as problematical; but they were exceptions. Most historians held an implicit, unquestioning faith in the power of ideas in history and consequently felt no need to analyze them. On the other hand, the so-called scientific historians who came to the fore in the late nineteenth century were so distrustful of idealism and subjectivity that they too neglected the history of ideas. The great expansion of intellectual history and its consequent development into one of the main genres of American historical scholarship did not occur until the autonomy of mind became in the twentieth century a crucial issue in contemporary culture. When man's capacity to shape his destiny by taking thought seemed terribly important yet also precarious and vulnerable, the study of intellectual history flowered. We have here an apparent, though not a real, paradox. Up to a point, the spread of intellectual history accompanied the breakdown of an older faith in the supremacy of ideas.

The curious association between an idealistic philosophy of history and a neglect of the history of ideas appears strikingly in the leading American historians of the mid-nineteenth century. A cheerful assurance that ideas rule the world was then at a high point. The principal historian of the United States, George Bancroft, was probably more gifted than any of his contemporaries in tracing the interplay between currents of thought. Except for a few brilliant passages, however, Bancroft's *History of the United States of America* presented a narrative of discovery, heroes, and public affairs. Bancroft apparently assumed that spiritual forces project themselves so transparently through all events and institutions as to require only occasional separate treatment. "Principles grow into life by informing the public mind," Bancroft grandly declared, "and in their maturity gain the mastery over events; following each other as they are bidden, and ruling without a pause. No sooner do the agitated waves begin to subside, than, amidst the formless tossing of the billows, a new messenger from the Infinite Spirit moves over the waters; and the bark which is freighted with the fortunes of mankind yields to the gentle breath."[1] The omnipotence of ideas need only be invoked, not demonstrated.

Romantic historians like Bancroft saw the ideas of men as mere extensions or complications of the Ideas of the Infinite Spirit. The beginnings of a broadly conceived intellectual history lie farther back, among writers for whom man's intellectual activity had no cosmic guarantee but was desperately important. Led by Voltaire, philosophers in the second half of the eighteenth century created a kind of history that tried to appraise the progress of civilization by emphasizing accomplishments in the arts, the sciences, and other refinements of living. For these Enlightenment writers the record of cultural achievement provided the best evidence of the power of reason, the best assurance of man's ability to struggle out of barbarism and ignorance. But the evidence was scattered, intellectual progress was far from cumulative. History in very large measure remained a spectacle of crimes and follies. Thus the history of civilization deserved close and anxious scrutiny. It was a testing ground for the Enlightenment's theory of progress.[2]

The first systematic study of intellectual history by an American addressed itself directly to the problem the Enlightenment posed. Samuel Miller was a Presbyterian clergyman in New York City, a devout Calvinist who nonetheless adhered to Thomas Jefferson and moved in the worldly literary circle of the Friendly Club. At the dawn of the nineteenth century the Reverend Miller preached a sermon on the leading tendencies of the century just past. The subject took hold of him, and the sermon grew into a two-volume work, *A Brief Retrospect of the Eighteenth Century* (1803), which offered a detailed conspectus of "revolutions and improvements" in the arts, in every field of knowledge, in education, and even in popular culture, both in Europe and in the United States. Throughout, Miller relentlessly pursued one central question: how much real progress has mankind effected in spite of the infidelity of the age and the insurmountable limitations on human nature? Mediating between

Christianity and the secular hopes of the Enlightenment, Miller's conclusions were temperate and balanced. He rejected extravagant notions of perfectibility while hailing the unprecedented "mass of improvement" that flowed from reason, experiment, and free inquiry. The record of intellectual achievement furnished Miller with an array of careful distinctions. He could specify the gains made in various provinces of thought, and the substantial benefits they entailed, while preserving a cautious attitude toward the slower, more uncertain progress of virtue.[3] For subtlety and judiciousness *A Brief Retrospect* still merits our admiration.

Miller published the book in his early thirties. He never fufilled an original intention to add another volume on theology, morals, and political theory. In later years, this Jeffersonian clergyman quit New York City, retreated to the Princeton Theological Seminary, and regretted the liberal rationalism of his youth.[4] So, in a different way, did the people for whom he wrote. After the age of reason passed, a faith in progress became for most Americans so vastly inflated—so confidently grounded in a sense of invincible national destiny—that specifically intellectual activity seemed much less important as a propelling force. The study of intellectual history languished until, in the late nineteenth century, a new conflict between science and religion reopened the question the Enlightenment posed. Once again the direction of history provided a crucial test of the power of reason.

In the nineteenth century formal historical writing ran heavily toward politics and institutions. Although a profoundly historical spirit gradually penetrated every domain of consciousness, just a small number of remarkable books established in the second half of the century the classic standards for writing intellectual history in the Anglo-American world. These books resumed, with greater system and sophistication, the eighteenth-century study of the influence of reason on the progress of culture. Henry T. Buckle's *History of Civilization in England* (2 vols., 1857–61) was directly and consciously in the tradition of Voltaire. Buckle tried to prove that every forward step in civilization—every improvement in religion, literature, government, and the condition of society—flowed from the accumulation and diffusion of empirical knowledge. In America John W. Draper's *History of the Intellectual Development of Europe* (1861) paralleled and supplemented Buckle's argument. Both men, in the spirit of the Enlightenment, defined progress as the victory of rational skepticism over religious superstition. Buckle's work prepared the way in Britain for the less ambitious but richer, more enduring works of W. E. H. Lecky and Leslie Stephen.[5] In Lecky's *History of the Rise and Influence of the Spirit of Rationalism in Europe* (2 vols., 1865) and in Stephen's *History of English Thought in the Eighteenth Century* (2 vols., 1876) the advance of a scientific world-view remained the central theme. But it was now stated with restraint and complexity in a finely wrought narrative.

Certain differences between Buckle on the one hand and Lecky and Stephen on the other foreshadow later contrasts in approach to intellectual history. Buckle called his book a history of civilization because he was writing about the relation of intellectual activity to the total history in which it occurred. Accordingly, he dealt with external culture as much as with ideas. Also, he dwelled on general conditions, taking very little account of individuals. Lecky and Stephen described their work as the history of thought or of opinion because their interest was in a closer inspection of changing ideas. They regarded Buckle as deficient in the power to project himself into the minds of other men and ages; and while they endeavored to take account of the whole inner life of a period or a nation, they attached a special significance to the thinking of outstanding individuals.[6] They surpassed Buckle in the ability to analyze ideas; but in doing so they restricted the range of their subject.

In spite of differences in scope and level of inquiry, the Victorians who reawakened interest in intellectual history had much in common. All of them were rationalists, enlisted in the late nineteenth century "warfare" between science and religion. In one sense, their books were histories of that warfare, histories that measured "the march of intellect" in terms of its emancipation from arbitrary theologies and oppressive institutions.[7] They were also much more than that. The pioneers of the new intellectual history possessed conceptual resources that enabled them to address further objectives, well beyond the reach of the Enlightenment.

Buckle to a limited extent and his successors to a much greater degree were imbued with a characteristically nineteenth century sense of all the all-encompassing interrelatedness of the historical process. Intellect was not just a deus ex machina pushing civilization forward, it was also a product of social evolution. Thus an intricate web of reciprocal connections could lead the historian's attention from ideas to their milieu or environment and back again. "It is impossible," Lecky remarked, "to lay down a railway without creating an intellectual influence."[8] In addition to assessing the quality of a civilization by evaluating the nature and implications of its intellectual products, historians should trace the manifold influence linking those products to the circumstances of their time.

Furthermore, the recognition that all of man's beliefs are caught up in the flux of history inspired in Lecky and Stephen a special interest in the inter-connections between ideas. If no belief is fixed or final, theist and agnostic might at least agree on seeking guidance from the underlying direction of intellectual change. In that grand, evolutionary movement of "the collective wisdom of mankind," individual opinions may be—as Lecky said—"but the eddies of an advancing stream." Intellectual history shows us the main current. It alone can disclose "that hidden bias of the imagination which—deeper than any strife of arguments, deeper than any change of creed—determines in each succeeding age the realized belief." The distinctive task of intellectual history, therefore, became one of describing and explaining the spirit of an age. That spirit, informing its formal philosophies and its practical activities, could be discovered by examining a variety of articulate representatives and determining their distinctive "mental habits" or their common "cast of mind."[9] In such fashion intellectual history supplied an evolutionary substitute for the old certainties that were fading from religion and philosophy.

In summary, what is today called intellectual history manifested itself in the nineteenth century in a relatively dense form as the history of civilization and, at a more rarified level, as the history of thought. It had also acquired three basic objectives that have shaped its subsequent development. Then and now, intellectual history estimates the changing level of intellectual achievement; relates thinking to behavior; and defines the patterns of feeling and opinion which, on the most extended scale, make up the spirit of an age or of a people.

On the methodological questions that became so perplexing later—questions of what qualifies as thought, and how it interacts with events—the nineteenth-century intellectual historians maintained a serene and deliberate vagueness. These questions did not trouble them very much. An organic theory of culture, which they took for granted, decreed that the relations between thought and deed must be intimate; and their own desire to face the great issues of their time in terms of fundamental principles insured that their history would emphasize serious and substantial types of expression, approached from a non-technical point of view. The traditional intellectual historians now seem naive in their evolutionary assumptions, and their selection of materials was generally more limited than their intentions.[10] Yet they did important work, on a spacious scale, with the aid of a clear purpose.

## II

Some distinguished intellectual history was written in the United States before the First World War, but strikingly little of it dealt with America. Although some of the principal innovators were keenly interested in the history of their own country, when they turned to it they reverted to the study of politics and institutions rather than ideas. After sketching the "intellectual development" of Europe, John W. Draper published a strictly political and military history of the Civil War. In the next generation, the famous Columbia University scholar, William A. Dunning, produced a magisterial history of political thought in Europe. At the same time, in American history, he sired a school of historians who scorned the "abstract theories" of the idealists and focused on allegedly practical necessities.[11] Perhaps the most interesting case is that of Henry Adams, who wrote brilliantly on medieval culture and also on early American politics. In both instances Adams tried to put his subject in an intellectual context. His *Mont-Saint-Michel and Chartres* (1905) succeeded; but the descriptions of intellectual life in the introductory and concluding chapters of the *History of the United States during the Administrations of Jefferson and Madison* (9 vols., 1889–91), artful as they were in their own right, had no connection with the intervening political narrative, and Adams knew it. "Readers will be troubled, at almost every chapter of the coming narrative," he cautioned, "by want of some formula to explain what share the popular imagination bore in the system pursued by government."[12]

Clearly, the American past failed to inspire the historians of culture and ideas. There were, to be sure, exceptions; one thinks of George Santayana's dazzling essay, "The Genteel Tradition in American Philosophy."[13] But these were not major works, and it may be significant that they were sometimes—as in the case of Santayana's essay—exercises in denigration. Evidently the paucity of systematic speculation and the small number of major thinkers in the American past discouraged historical investigation. By the late nineteenth century, "culture" had come to mean something rarified, genteel, remote from everyday life.[14] In the world of the gentleman-scholar it was an embarrassment that America had relatively little of it. Samuel Miller in 1803 had been proud of the cultural advances America was making and gave special attention to them; but the historians of the Gilded Age generally thought of culture as belonging chiefly to Europe. Other intellectual historians must have shared the belief of the great American medievalist, Henry Osborn Taylor, that American civilization was too practical and unlovely to warrant attention.[15]

To find substance and significance in American intellectual life under these conditions a historian would need what Henry Adams together with most of the gentlemen of his day signally lacked: a conviction of the vitality and importance of "the popular imagination." Two self-taught scholars who were possessed by that conviction inaugurated the critical study of American intellectual history. Moses Coit Tyler and Edward Eggleston differed from one another in numerous ways. Tyler wrote the history of thought; Eggleston devoted himself to the history of civilization. But both men were inspired rather than repelled or troubled by the democratic openness of American culture. Both grew up in plain, midwestern communities, Tyler in Michigan, Eggleston in southern Indiana, and as young men both lived in a state of almost constant mobility. Both conceived of intellectual history as the study not of an elite but of a variegated multitude.

Tyler escaped the usual cultural snobbery of his day primarily because of a fervent belief in the enduring worthiness of the spirit and ideals of early America. It is helpful to think of him as a latter-day Emersonian, shaped by the antebellum reform movements, fired by the idealistic nationalism of Charles Sumner, but turning to history rather than prophecy to invoke the continuing vitality of the American dream. Tyler had been ordained into the Congregational ministry before the Civil War, and after it he sought an alternative means of providing guidance and inspiration for an age that seemed morally adrift. Alarmed at the growth of materialism, corruption, and skepticism, Tyler found in the vocation of the scholar a way of using "'tongue and pen,'" as he remarked, "to help American civilization to be a success." His pioneering *A History of American Literature, 1607–1765* (2 vols., 1878) and its sequel, *The Literary History of the American Revolution, 1763–1783* (2 vols., 1897) were intended, Tyler said, to illustrate "the majestic operation of ideas, the creative and decisive play of spiritual forces, in the development of history."[16]

Majestic though they might be, Tyler's spiritual forces revealed in his pages very little subtlety of content or doctrine. He never dug deeply into what he called "the sublime and hideous dogmas"[17] of New England Puritanism. Basically he presented a sequence of writers rather than a system of thought, and he dwelled on the immediate circumstances in which they lived rather than the intellectual influences on which they drew. What really interested Tyler was the way men held and expressed their convictions, the uses they made of them. His aim was literary as well as historical; but he was unapologetic about exhuming dozens of obscure writers of no aesthetic merit, for they seemed to him to give voice to the emotions and aspirations that stirred the rank and file of the American people. Although he was in some ways a conservative man, Tyler came to intellectual history with vivid, eclectic sympathies. One can understand the judgment of a contemporary critic who said that the main impression Tyler's work left was of "a more profound sense of the part democracy has played in American life and culture."[18]

Though Edward Eggleston never struck the inspirational note that resounded through Tyler's writing, Eggleston's democratic sympathies were at least as broad. Moreover, his view of the historical process was wider and more complex. In the divergence between these two American historians, we may observe some of the differences that were developing also in Europe between the history of thought and the history of civilization. As a historian of ideas, Tyler studied the spirit of an age as revealed in the beliefs of individuals. He was happy to find in Buckle a convincing demonstration that the spirit of an age rules its outward events; but he was too much of an Emersonian individualist to accept the other side of Buckle, the side that championed science, technological progress, modernity, and viewed history as an impersonal process of cause and effect. Eggleston, on the other hand, shared Buckle's interest in the scientific study of social evolution. Like Buckle, Eggleston ignored individuals and looked instead for direct evidence of the collective mentality of a people. Whereas Tyler emphasized the generative power of beliefs, Eggleston stressed the resistance to progress arising from ignorance, superstition, and environment. While Tyler conceived of his work as a history of ideas, Eggleston accurately described his as a history of civilization.[19]

Eggleston's one enduring historical work, *The Transit of Civilization from England to America in the Seventeenth Century* (1901), ranged widely across the folklore, the moral standards, the crude cosmological notions, the educational practices, and the religious habits of the early colonists. Insistently Eggleston pointed at the backwardness of the age. (The contrast he intended, between the stagnation of the seventeenth century and the progress to be attained in later eras through scientific knowledge, would undoubtedly have been elaborated in subsequent volumes, but he did not live to write them.) Nevertheless, the book was far from being a polemic. Eggleston brought from his earlier career as a literary realist of the "local-color" school a keen, delighted eye for the homespun life of ordinary people, benighted though they might be; and this gave his history authenticity and charm.

Its principal shortcoming was not so much in Eggleston's bias as in his inability to sustain a consistent point of view. On the one hand, he wanted to show that the American colonists clung tenaciously to the popular culture of Elizabethan England. On the other hand, he saw that the new environment wrought major changes, not always for the better. Unable to integrate the two perspectives, he oscillated between them. When Eggleston's book was published in 1901, Frederick Jackson Turner and his followers were already establishing a simple, single-minded conception of the predominance of environment over cultural inheritance. Probably because it did not fit the Turnerian mold, *The Transit of Civilization* fell into an unfortunate neglect.

Indeed, the whole enterprise of intellectual history suffered a temporary check in the early twentieth century, as the great amateurs who had opened and defined the subject gave way to scholars enclosed in particular academic disciplines. Intellectual history had been created by men who were striving to maintain a unified worldview. It could not flourish easily among professors who were busily building academic fences and arranging separate jurisdictions. Most of the early professional historians were institutionalists. They deliberately restricted their attention to the history of legal and constitutional structures, those substantial foundations of national authority on which a conservative elite could place its faith in stability. A few of the institutional historians, notably those trained in law, did study a part of the history of ideas. Charles H. McIlwain, Edward S. Corwin, and Andrew C. McLaughlin traced with loving discrimination the slow unfolding of the ideas underlying the American Constitution.[20] But these men were unusual. Mostly the institutionalists stayed on more solid ground. Their primary interest was in the relation between events and the formal structure of authority.

Many of them seem to have distrusted intellectual history as a quagmire of subjectivity.

Among professional historians, dissatisfaction with these cautious, separatist attitudes soon broke out, and it was within the rebellious minority, who felt stultified by the predominant ethos of their profession, that a new interest in intellectual history awakened. James Harvey Robinson, who taught European history at Columbia University, had a crusading passion to make history once again relevant to contemporary problems. A growing divorce between history and the new social sciences was threatening the primacy of an historical approach to the study of man. Reacting against this separation, Robinson wanted professional historians to widen their scope, join hands with social scientists, and bring their knowledge to bear on current issues. Robinson called this the "New History." As Robert Skotheim has pointed out, however, it was a modified, up-dated version of Buckle's attempt to make history the science of social evolution.[21] In a still larger perspective, Robinson was carrying into the twentieth century the Voltairean conception of a comprehensive history of civilization, which would chart man's progress in terms of the triumphs and achievements of reason.

Robinson's scheme of things also allowed a special place for intellectual history in the narrower sense of the history of thought. We should study intellectual history, Robinson asserted, because it exposes the relativity of outmoded beliefs and thus helps us to bring our own opinions up to date. Ideas change more slowly than the environments in which they take form. By studying the vicissitudes of past opinion, we can learn to adapt our ideas to our present environment. Such was the guiding principle behind an immensely influential course Robinson inaugurated in 1904, "Intellectual History of Western Europe." It unsettled the hallowed beliefs of many students, among whom it was informally dubbed "The Downfall of Christianity."[22]

Although Robinson had a profound impact on scholarship as well as teaching, his approach to intellectual history did not in itself prove wholly encouraging. If changes in thought are assumed ordinarily to lag behind changes in environmental conditions, should not historians concentrate on environment rather than ideas? That was also an implication easily drawn from Turner's emphasis on the natural environment, and especially in the field of American history it was exactly what Robinson's early followers did. Charles A. Beard's iconoclastic studies of the Founding Fathers and the Jeffersonians described their ideas, but only sufficiently to substantiate the subordination of political theories to material circumstances.[23] Beard did not suppose that the ideas themselves presented any serious interpretive challenge. To put mental activity in the center of attention, and thus to resume the work of Tyler and Eggleston, professional scholars would need some further incentive beyond the ambivalent teachings of James Harvey Robinson.

### III

Around the time of the First World War a great deal that Americans had taken for granted about themselves came into question. Nearly everyone had assumed throughout the nineteenth and early twentieth centuries that a set of readily comprehensible ideals undergirded the United States and gave it a special destiny. The ideals were simple and essentially congenial to human nature. The difficult, important questions had to do with their application rather than their substance or survival. On the eve of the First World War a fundamental reexamination of these national pieties began. The skepticism that had earlier assailed religious absolutes inspired the intellectual history written in the second half of the nineteenth century. Now skepticism extended to American national traditions, and a much wider realm of values was thrown open to historical scrutiny. "It is amazing," Van Wyck Brooks wrote in 1918, "how that fabric of ideas and assumptions, of sentiments and memories and attitudes which made up the civilization of our fathers has melted away like snow uncovering the sordid facts of a society that seems to us now so little advanced on the path of spiritual evolution."[24] We must, Brooks insisted, reconstruct our literary and intellectual history. We need a new, "usable past."

As yet, Brooks' questioning had not shaken a nineteenth-century faith in progress: he could still, in 1918, refer casually to "the path of spiritual evolution." By the 1920's such comfortable formulas were beginning to sound old-fashioned. The belief that history tends generally toward the realization of American ideals certainly did not collapse in the years between the two world wars, but it could no longer be regarded as a self-evident truth. Accordingly, the critical examination of American traditions inaugurated in the Progressive Era became also an inquiry into the direction in which they were developing. The full urgency of the study of intellectual history began to be felt as intellectuals became aware that the unsettlement of traditional beliefs could not automatically be defined as progress in the manner of James Harvey Robinson. A number of literary intellectuals thereupon followed Brooks's lead in reexamining American ideals. The informal kind of intellectual history written from many different perspectives by D. H. Lawrence in *Studies in Classic American Literature* (1923), by William Carlos Williams in *In the American Grain* (1925), by Lewis Mumford in *The Golden Day* (1926), by Constance Rourke in *American Humor* (1931), by James Truslow Adams in *The Epic of America* (1931), and by Granville Hicks in *The Great Tradition* (1933) was in each case an effort to discover the roots of a living culture, a culture capable of further growth in the midst of desiccation.[25]

The first work of serious historical scholarship in which this postwar ferment came to expression was Carl Becker's *The Declaration of Independence: A Study in the History of Political Ideas* (1922). Becker had studied under Robinson at Columbia and had absorbed Robinson's interest in intellectual history as a dissolvent of traditional, unscientific ideas. Becker differed from most of the New Historians, however, in having little confidence that scientific progress was providing a more humane and reliable framework of belief. Less cheerfully empirical than his professional colleagues, more speculative and troubled than they, Becker was deeply affected by the disillusion that followed World War I. He studied the history of thought to determine whether his own rationalistic world view and his own underlying commitment to progress were still viable. His conclusions were shocking; they were also exciting. Turning back to the Enlightenment, the seedbed of his own heritage, Becker in *The Declaration of Independence* described the basic articles of the American Creed as expressions of an obsolete climate of opinion. In some ways the eighteenth century's reliance on Natural Law seemed more in tune with the rationalism of the Middle Ages than with "the harsh realities of the modern world." These realities, Becker sadly concluded, have "provided an atmosphere in which faith in Humanity could only gasp for breath."[26]

Unique in the depth of his disillusionment, Becker was unique also among professional historians in the 1920's in the philosophic breadth of his approach to the history of ideas. Becker demonstrated anew the value of studying changing "climates of opinion"—to use a phrase he borrowed from the philosopher Alfred North White-head—as a means of clarifying one's own beliefs and estimating their staying power.[27] This was the tradition of Lecky, of Stephen, and to a lesser degree of Moses Coit Tyler; and in the 1920's it was powerfully revived by Whitehead's *Science and the Modern World* (1925). But Becker's interests shifted more and more to European history. Philosophers with historical tastes were largely preoccupied with European materials too.[28] It remained for an obscure professor of English at the University of Washington to write the first pano-ramic history of the whole sweep of American thought.

In important respects, Vernon L. Parrington walked in the foot-steps of Moses Coit Tyler. Parrington too was a plain midwesterner, raised in the same Victorian atmosphere of piety, moral earnestness, and cultural aspiration. Although his religion dropped away in college, a related zeal for the spiritual and cultural redemption of America was never slaked. Intellectual history gave Parrington the same means that Tyler had chosen for exercising that zeal. Both men found a vocation in fighting the tawdry materialism of their own time by summoning forth the idealistic principles at work in history. Characteristically, Parrington entitled the first draft of his magnum opus, "The Democratic Spirit in American Letters."[29] Moreover, he obviously felt, as Tyler had, the importance of indi-viduals as carriers and exponents of ideas. Adopting the strategy that Tyler had used, Parrington constructed his book as a series of biographical vignettes of American writers. In each of these sketches the character, the energy, and the moral stance of the man count fully as much as his ideas. Parrington simply went a step or two beyond Tyler by pitting the chief characters against one another in a continuing ideological warfare, liberal heroes versus conservative villains, and by enclosing the whole story in an elaborate interpretive framework.

These latter features reflected the influence of the new historians and the younger cultural critics. Parrington enthusiastically embraced their reformist aims. He adopted also their skeptical, environmentalist attitudes. Like them, he needed to strip the veil of gentility from American literature. He needed to rediscover a "usable past" in the hurly-burly of social conflict. Whereas Tyler was content to reaffirm a national faith, Parrington wanted also to expose the illusions and obstacles perplexing it and to discover the direction of its development. He undertook, as he confessed, "in the spirit of the Enlightenment . . . a reexamination of the American past in order to forecast an ampler democratic future."[30] The result, published as *Main Currents in American Thought* in two volumes in 1927 and a posthumous third in 1930, was a powerful but volatile amalgam. It answered all of the objectives of intellectual history; it fused all of the strands that had gone into the subject. Much of the strength of the book, and also some of its weaknesses, arose from the conflation of two styles of scholarship. The older style was spacious, lofty, and humane; the new style was probing, corrosive, and realistic.

In striving for epic scale, Parrington took tremendous risks in interpretation, risks that a more academic man (Parrington had only a B.A.) could not have accepted. Basically, however, his interpretive pattern rested on the New History of Turner and Beard. Lifelong experience as a westerner, rebuffed or ignored by the citadels of eastern culture, predisposed Parrington in favor of Turner's frontier hypothesis. The frontier was, Parrington agreed, the master force in nourishing the ideals that are most deeply American. For explaining changes in those ideals, he found the emphasis Beard put on conflict between economic classes especially useful. Parrington therefore blended the two environmentalisms, one geographical, the other economic. He grouped his characters as much as possible according to region, thereby suggesting the importance of sectional identification. Then, within each section, Parrington arrayed men against one another in accordance with contrasting socioeconomic allegiances. In New England it was Puritan elite versus homespun separatists; in the South, Jeffersonian democrats versus the aristocracy of South Carolina; in the West, Jacksonian farmers against Whig capitalists.

Parrington manipulated his complex dichotomies with a perilous virtuosity that was close to sleight of hand. His scheme took on a certain architectonic grandeur, for its manifold social dualisms were interlinked by the "main currents" of thought. The currents expressed a persistent ideological contrast. In spite of much branching and proliferation, one current carried democratic tendencies, the other carried antidemocratic tendencies. Both of them (the antidemocratic current especially) were shaped, guided, and supported by the social contexts and antagonisms through which they flowed. But they were not entirely dependent on any social matrix. Parrington's intellectual history seemed alive because the currents laced it with energies arising outside of particular American environments. Instead of starting from a native setting, the currents stemmed initially from certain English, French, and German ideas. Thus Parrington offset the environmentalism of Turner and Beard with a more traditional attention to the European origins of American culture. In doing so he depicted powerful intellectual systems capable of penetrating the environments that reacted upon them. His grand design provided for an intricate balance between European heritage and American environment, just as it counterposed individuals to social groups. Both polarities reflected a deeper conflict in Parrington's mind between ideals and material "realities."

Parrington could never resolve that underlying tension; he could never reconcile or integrate what he strove constantly to balance. The issue obsessed him, for the critical and realistic side of his own outlook threatened to undercut his ideals. In writing *Main Currents* he had set out to "forecast an ampler democratic future," but he soon found himself asking the same question that troubled Becker. Can

American ideals flourish and develop amid "the harsh realities of the modern world"? Although Parrington refused to be altogether pessimistic, disillusion shadowed the third volume of *Main Currents*. American democracy, he believed, required a Jeffersonian confidence that reason and education can progressively supersede coercion in human affairs. Yet modern science was more and more revealing the limits of freedom and rationality. Man's rational self-determination seemed more and more an illusion. Was not American thought, after breaking free in the eighteenth and early nineteenth centuries from an older kind of determinism, slipping back into a naturalistic determinism in the twentieth century?

If we recall that the Anglo-American tradition of writing intellectual history had grown from a need to test the large claims the Enlightenment made for the influence of intellect in history, the fascination Parrington's magnum opus exerted upon a whole generation of students becomes quite understandable. During the years between the two world wars the crucial values of the Enlightenment—reason, individual freedom, progress—were challenged as never before in American experience. Parrington wrote history that was simultaneously a rousing invocation of those values and an intimation of their declining power. To take up the problems he posed became one of the most exciting ways of discovering a usable past.

## IV

Within the historical profession the period between the two world wars was the heyday of the New History. It was also the birthtime of a profound reaction against some aspects of the New History, particularly against the environmental determinism that presented ideas as lingering after-effects of material conditions. Gradually the New Historians modified their assumption of the primacy of external reality. Other scholars insisted on the pre-eminent—or at least the privileged—role of ideas in history. Both groups contributed to an extraordinary growth of interest during the 1930's and 1940's in the study of American intellectual history.

During the same year that Parrington published the first two volumes of *Main Currents,* Charles A. Beard brought out another of the great progressive syntheses, *The Rise of American Civilization* (2 vols., 1927). In that panoramic work, written with the collaboration of his wife, Beard extended across the whole span of American history the economic interpretation he had earlier applied to the political issues of the late eighteenth century. He continued to subordinate ideas to "interests." But Beard also had another purpose in writing *The Rise of American Civilization.* Against the postwar prophets of disillusion, against the Spenglerian pessimists and the popular debunkers, he wanted to demonstrate the vitality of American culture. He wanted to affirm its unexhausted potentialities. For the first time a general survey of United States history incorporated prominent strands of intellectual development. Moreover, Beard's own values—science, education, secularism, social democracy, faith in progress—were presented as dynamic causes of historical changes, not mere effects of material environments. Beard wrote with a confidence that Parrington and Becker lacked. Nevertheless, he too turned to intellectual history with acute concern over the apparent contradiction between his ideals and his conception of reality. He too sought assurance from history that man can overcome existing realities by taking thought.

By entitling his work a history of civilization, Beard put himself squarely in the tradition of Voltaire and Buckle; and the introduction to the one-volume edition explicitly invoked their example. Like those great predecessors, Beard proposed to deal "with all the manifestations of the inner powers of a people, as well as the trappings of war and politics," thereby "suggesting capacities yet unexplored and hinting of emancipation from outward necessities."[31] One might say that Beard revived and refurbished the history of civilization, while Parrington in a very similar way modernized the history of ideas. Henceforth Beard attached great importance to the concept of civilization. In moving steadily away from economic determinism, he made "civilization" not just—or even primarily—an approach to history, but rather a moral standard. It became a kind of summary of the ideals emergent in American history.[32]

As a framework for studying American history, however, the concept of civilization proved unmanageable and fell into disuse. It tended to disguise what had become for professional historians the crucial problem of intellectual history, namely, the relation between thought and behavior. Preoccupation with that problem pushed into the background other questions that might fruitfully have been explored within the framework of the history of civilization. Instead, the New Historians' struggle to bridge the gap between mind and matter, to connect thought with deed in continuous interaction, produced a new genre known as "social and intellectual history." The name "social and intellectual" pointed up the underlying methodological issue and assigned to society a characteristic priority over thought. Arthur M. Schlesinger, a former student of Robinson and Beard at Columbia, inaugurated at Harvard in 1924 a famous course entitled "American Social and Intellectual History." It was copied far and wide with the aid of a thirteen-volume *History of American Life* (1927–48), which Schlesinger edited with the assistance of Dixon Ryan Fox. Schlesinger's own emphasis was upon social history, which he described as an endeavor "to distinguish between what men do and what they say" and thus disclose "the realities that underlie the rationalizations."[33] On the other hand, Merle Curti, a somewhat younger admirer of Beard, concentrated on ideas. Yet he also interpreted them consistently as functional to patterns of behavior.

Attention to the interplay of thought and action encouraged a special interest in the dissemination of ideas through various levels of society. In any given situation, what is the connection between popular culture and an intellectual elite? Here was an attractive way of looking closely at linkages between ideas and events. Moreover, the study of popular thought gave intellectual history a democratic flavor. New Historians had the authority of John Dewey for believing that an undemocratic class structure had kept traditional philosophy aloof from the needs and interests of ordinary people. On the same premise they might suspect that the older history of ideas was aristocratic, and out of place in an age of science and democracy.[34] In spite of the reductionistic tendency of such views, a very wide-spectrumed history, bringing together the study of a high culture, popular thought, and social context, was probably the most considerable achievement of the followers of Beard and Turner in the interwar period. The achievement was crowned in 1943 with Merle Curti's *The Growth of American Thought,* a work of truly extraordinary scope, which remains the most comprehensive treatment of the subject.

Yet the essential problem that baffled Parrington and Beard persisted unsolved. Indeed, it could not be solved; it was rooted in incompatible assumptions. As realists, influenced by materialistic interpretations of history, the New Historians supposed that ideas are functionally subordinate to interests. They usually concluded, as Richard Hofstadter did of Social Darwinism, that "changes in the structure of social ideas wait on general changes in economic and political life."[35] On the other hand, as reformers, they counted ultimately on the life of reason to remake society. How to reconcile a "realistic" conviction that behavior precedes ideas with an enlightened reliance on intellect as the engine of progress? How to avoid going round in circles, continually distinguishing between ideas and interests only to mix them together?

Preoccupation with functional relationships inevitably interfered with a sustained analysis of ideas; and so did the concomitant interest in widening the contextual range of historical narrative. The study of intellectual history gained rapidly in popularity; but two of its traditional objectives—appraising the level of intellectual achievement and describing the spirit of an age—were neglected. Some of the coherence of the older history of ideas was dissipated. By the 1940's Beard, Schlesinger, Curti, and a good many of their students and associates were taking more account of the quality of thought, trying to do more justice to the interior of ideas.[36] But already an outright rebellion against the presuppositions of the New History had started in the 1930's.

The rebellion broke out simultaneously in several humanistic disciplines. One stream of influence flowed from Arthur O. Lovejoy, a Johns Hopkins philosopher renowned for his criticism of pragmatism and realism. Lovejoy developed a subtle, very impressive technique for tracing the influence of philosophical ideas in other provinces of thought, particularly in literature. His chief book, *The Great Chain of Being: A Study of the History of an Idea* (1936), traced a cluster of "unit-ideas," as he called them—in contrast to complex intellectual systems—from Plato to the German Romantics. His interest was not at all in the socioeconomic conditioning of these primordial ideas, or in their impact on events, but rather in their interweaving with one another and their spread through otherwise diverse bodies of literature, science, and theology. Lovejoy conceived of his scrupulous attention to logical connections and quasi-rational affinities in the history of thought as counterbalancing the excesses of psychological and social interpretation. "It must still be admitted," Lovejoy declared, "that philosophers (and even plain men) *do* reason, that the temporal sequence of their reasonings, as one thinker follows another, is usually in some considerable degree a logically motivated and logically instructive sequence."[37] Although very few of Lovejoy's many disciples worked in American intellectual history, indirectly the influence of his writings and of *The Journal of the History of Ideas,* which he founded in 1940, was not negligible.

Another current stemmed from professors at Harvard and Yale who were involved in joint programs in history and literature. At Yale Ralph Gabriel grew dissatisfied with what he regarded as the intellectual confusion and the overblown pretensions of the social sciences and their ally, the New History.[38] His pioneering synthesis, *The Course of American Democratic Thought* (1940), argued that certain fundamental ideas had survived largely unchanged through all the social upheavals of the nineteenth and twentieth centuries.

At Harvard the reaction began as a defense of the early American Puritans against the disparaging economic interpretations of Parrington and James Truslow Adams. In 1926 Samuel Eliot Morison was appointed official historian of Harvard University in preparation for its three hundredth anniversary ten years later. Already an authority on New England in the eighteenth century, Morison threw all of his great zest into a study of the founders of Massachusetts. A series of books, beginning with *Builders of the Bay Colony*

(1930), depicted Puritanism as a dynamic force impelled by intellectual and spiritual vitality.[39] A young colleague in the Department of English, Perry Miller, soon joined Morison—and before long surpassed him—in attributing the institutions of the Puritans to their religious beliefs. "I have attempted," Miller declared grandly in the preface to his first book, "to tell of a great folk movement with an utter disregard of the social and economic factors."[40] Instead, he argued that the Puritans carried unchanged to America a conceptual scheme already worked out in Europe. Miller described that conceptual scheme with great erudition and power of analysis in *The New England Mind: The Seventeenth Century* (1939).

What Lovejoy, Gabriel, Morison, and Miller shared was not just a humanistic bent and an accompanying belief in the importance of ideas. They were also reacting strongly against the environmental determinism that constituted one side of the New History. In their own approach to intellectual history, a body of beliefs initiates the sequence of action. Whereas New Historians tended to see men as *adapting* (or failing to adapt) to their environment, these revisionists saw men as *intervening* in an environment or a situation. More or less explicitly, they celebrated the struggle of human consciousness and will against the coercions of fate. Thus Gabriel presented the idea of the untrammeled individual as the "central affirmation" in "the American democratic faith." Over against it he counterposed a succession of determinisms. Morison, to the surprise of most readers, argued that the Puritans were not predestinarian Calvinists. Heroic activists, they believed that salvation lay within the reach of every person who made an effort.[41] Perry Miller's more subtle and authentic portrait discovered a Puritanism internally divided between a passionate demand for freedom and an unflinching recognition of necessity. Miller's books about the Puritans were charged with his own sense of the excitement and ardor of a life of sustained intellectual initiative in a cosmos man cannot master or more than superficially comprehend.[42] Thus the revisionists wrestled with the same dilemma—the opposition between humanistic ideals and external realities—that perplexed the New History. Haunted by the vision of a deterministic universe, Miller had more in common with

Parrington than he himself was inclined to recognize. Indeed, the whole of American culture in the 1930's and early 1940's was pervaded by the issue that simultaneously divided and united the students of intellectual history. A time of hard-boiled materialism on the one hand, it was also an age committed to bring reason and idealism to bear on the course of history. The study of intellectual history flourished as a way of asking how far that was possible.

At the time, the influence of the New Historians predominated in the historical profession. Miller, for example, was not widely read until after World War II. It was, however, the revisionist approach to the role of ideas in history that survived and flourished in the postwar era. New Historians worked under the spur of a theory of progress which they could neither renounce nor consistently accept. Gradually the spur became a handicap, for progress seemed less and less plausible with every passing year. From Samuel Miller to Merle Curti most writers of American intellectual history wanted to find that the general tendency of history was favorable to their own values. Fundamentally, they counted on an increasing power of rationality in human affairs. As we have already observed, the history progressive historians wrote when their faith was challenged after World War I brought little reassurance. In the doomsday world of the 1940's this kind of faith in history disintegrated.

The revisionists had never relied on progress. They had never expected the course of history to vindicate their values. They did not imagine their own world—or what they could anticipate in the future—to be any great improvement over the past they wrote about. Consequently they escaped the progressive historians' tendency to appraise ideas instrumentally. The theory of progress led historians to understand ideas as plans of action, to be judged according to a programmatic outcome. It encouraged a classification of ideas as either progressive or conservative, either assisting or retarding social evolution. Gabriel and Perry Miller, on the other hand, were free to explore conflicts and ambiguities within an intellectual system, without having to pit it against another body of ideas or decide what it contributed to social change.

Miller took the greatest advantage of that freedom. He opened up the tensions and cross-purposes within the mentality of early New England, finding there a richness and complexity that any theory of progress would necessarily have flattened and simplified. Instead of looking back from the vantage point of the present, as progressive scholars were inclined to do, perceiving Puritanism as an obstacle or a stage in the "rise" of modern ideas, Miller located himself inside the Puritan sensibility. His masterwork, *The New England Mind* (2 vols., 1939, 1953), expounded a total intellectual system having its own distinctive character and problems. Its significance he discovered not in what it might have "contributed" to social evolution but rather in its intricate engagement with perennial issues of human consciousness: feeling versus intellect, freedom versus necessity, mind versus matter.[43]

It may be said that Perry Miller—alone among recent American scholars—fulfilled all of the objectives of the intellectual historian. First, he gave an assessment of the quality of intellectual achievement in the periods he studied. (A high one it was, sometimes extravagantly so.) Secondly, after World War II he probed intensively into relations between thought and environment. While insisting on the initiative of mind he allowed also for the triumph of environment. Third, and most memorable, he described the spirit of an age, revealing its diversities as outgrowths of its unities. Yet Miller paid a price for operating without guidance from a theory of progress or any other general scheme of historical development. It was exceedingly difficult for his narrative to move from one intellectual system to another. After rooting himself in seventeenth century Puritanism, Miller told the story of its decline in the second volume of *The New England Mind* by continually pointing backward to what was breaking up. His frame of reference did not permit much pointing forward to what was forming. In subsequent writings he frequently interpreted aspects of eighteenth and nineteenth century thought as reenactments or revivals of earlier experience.[44] But his effort to pursue systematically "the meaning of America" had nowhere to go, for he never established a terminus ad quem. Tragically, Miller's later work splintered into fragments, as the Puritan system had done in his brilliant account of it.

## V

No one else was so ambitious. In many younger scholars who emerged after World War II, however, certain characteristics of Perry Miller's approach to the past became more obvious and emphatic. First, Miller was as much a student of literature as of history, having been associated with the Harvard program in history and literature from his first appointment as an instructor in 1931. Second, in contrast to Lovejoy's highly rationalistic attitude, Miller strained to do justice to the emotional side of history. He wrote with great intensity about feelings in order to convey their powerful bombardment of the intellect. Third, he became increasingly fascinated by the question of national character or national identity. In all of these respects Miller helped prepare the way for a new influence that impinged on the writing of American intellectual history in the 1940's and 1950's: the American Studies movement.

Institutionally, American Studies was a protest against confining specialization. Just as the New History a generation earlier had roused historians to break out of an orthodox political history, so the professors of American literature who were usually the prime movers in establishing American Studies programs were trying to break out of an orthodox literary history. Whereas the former group hoped to achieve a comprehensive view of the past, the latter sought an integrated view of American "civilization." Accordingly, the New Historians readily joined hands with their literary colleagues in sponsoring American Studies programs; but the aims of the two enterprises were by no means identical.[45]

The quest for breadth, which had inspired the New History, became in American Studies a pursuit of coherence: a search for a central meaning, or an explanatory method. It did not, therefore, revive the concept of an inclusive history of civilization. Instead, American Studies was experimental and essayistic. Moreover, the goal was not social reform as it had been with the New History, but rather the achievement of a national identity. After World War II the collapse of the idea of progress, together with the terrible anxieties and rigidities created by the Cold War, intensified among many people—liberal intellectuals as well as popular spokesmen—a need for an ideological foundation, a moral anchor. Perhaps it could be found by probing national traditions. In effect, the American Studies movement provided an academic base for prosecuting more actively the search for a "usable past" that had started among literary intellectuals around the time of the First World War.

By involving specialists in American literature in the study of intellectual history, American Studies introduced a new capability for close textual analysis. In contrast to the rather matter-of-fact approach of the New Historians, literary scholars were trained to look through and behind documents to grasp a man's thought. The methods of modern literary criticism enabled them to reach the ambiguous feelings and symbolic references that lurk beneath the surface of a historical document. When literary scholars began to apply the methods summarized in René Wellek and Austin Warren, *Theory of Literature* (1949), to materials other than conventional literary sources, they were in fact writing a new kind of intellectual history. This penetration in depth was first fully displayed in Henry Nash Smith's *Virgin Land* (1950), probably the most influential book that has come out of American Studies.

Smith's subtitle, *The American West as Symbol and Myth,* reflected his reliance on myth criticism, already a major preoccupation of American literary scholarship. In writing the history of symbols and myths, Smith and his successors broke out of the rationalistic view of man that had earlier dominated the study of American intellectual history. Since symbols are dramatic figures rather than purely denotative ideas, they can express paradoxical or ambivalent meanings. By rendering all ideas in pictorial terms, they serve to accommodate conflicting values and to bridge the various levels of rational discourse. In Smith's book, for example, the image of the "garden of the world" vividly unites Jeffersonian abstractions with popular fantasies about increased rainfall. The objective is a kind of analysis that fuses concept and emotion. This fusion is designed to bring the emotions into the foreground of intellectual history without destroying the framework of conceptual thought. But the conceptual side of intellectual life becomes largely a vehicle for the affective side.

This approach went a step beyond the revisionism of the 1930's in lifting the spell of the Enlightenment from the writing of intellectual history. Yet the perennial problem the Enlightenment had posed for intellectual historians was not put to rest; it was only reformulated. Intellectual historians still had to ask: what is the power of intellect in a world not wholly rational? The New History had addressed that problem by focusing on discordance between ideas and environment. After World War II the problem was internalized by writers who concentrated on relations between rational thought and impulse or fantasy.[46] They produced such notable studies of American mythology as John William Ward's *Andrew Jackson: Symbol for an Age* (1955), R. W. B. Lewis's *The American Adam* (1955), Harry Levin's *The Power of Blackness* (1958), William R. Taylor's *Cavalier and Yankee* (1961), and Leo Marx's *The Machine in the Garden* (1964).

Meanwhile, in the 1940's and 1950's, within the historical profession, the influence and popularity of intellectual history rose to an unprecedented level. A leading economic historian declared in 1948 that the profession's outstanding achievement in the last decade had been the invasion of the field of intellectual history. About the same time another senior scholar complained that only social history or the history of ideas seemed to attract the bright young men.[47] A good deal of this enthusiasm poured into specialized research on particular strands of thought. There were also major efforts by Stow Persons and Henry May to define periods in the history of ideas.[48] But the most striking development was the maturing of a generation of scholars who brought the methods and interests of intellectual history to bear on the major topics of American political and social history. Many differences separated Richard Hofstadter, C. Vann Woodward, Arthur M. Schlesinger, Jr., Edmund S. Morgan, Oscar Handlin, Daniel Boorstin, and David Donald. Yet all of them were rewriting American history—revising some part of the older progressive interpretation—by examining the mentalities of important groups and leaders.[49] Observing this phenomenon, Robert Skotheim commented: "American historians today seem to attach more importance to ideas in history than to histories of ideas."[50]

If the trend should continue, Skotheim speculated, intellectual historians might disappear, their work taken over by specialists in particular periods or themes. Possibly so. A great deal of healthy interpenetration has indeed occurred, with the result that distinctions between one range or level of history and another now seem less clear than they once did. Nevertheless, any complex culture that seeks guidance from the past cannot cease to ask itself the kinds of questions intellectual historians have wrestled with; and it would be rash to rely on general historians to do that. In some ways the tremendous vogue intellectual history acquired in the 1950's may be a hindrance in pursuing those questions. This is partly because of the nature of the vogue; partly also because of a current reaction against it.

Like their colleagues in American Studies, many of the leading historians of the 1950's were preeminently interested in the nonrational aspects of consciousness. More curious about feelings than ideas, they studied images, myths, anxieties, prejudices, fantasies, all with reference to the psychological dynamics of behavior. This valuable corrective to the rationalism of earlier scholarship was, of course, immensely fruitful and exciting. But the focus on emotional drives has perpetuated the professional historians' preoccupation with one of the objectives of intellectual history at the expense of the other two. Again the link between thought and behavior was highlighted, albeit in a new way. And again a fixation on that link (now through the study of motives) diverted attention both from intellectual achievement and from general patterns of thought. We still make little effort to appraise the quality of intellect or to mark its ebb and flow. It would, for example, be refreshing—but still almost unthinkable—to find American historians arguing over the relative merits of cultural endeavors at different points in time or in different locations. Motivational research (if I may call it that) also bypasses the problem of structure in intellectual history. An overriding emphasis on the feelings that flow directly into behavior gives small scope for studying intellectual systems or for uncovering the under-lying agreement that antagonists share. Any sustained effort to define the spirit of an age seems hardly worthwhile without an interest in the form of thought, as well as its energy.[51]

Of late we have seen an extraordinary volte-face on the historio-graphical issues of the 1950's. The American Studies movement has lost momentum. The quest for national identity—the interrogation of the "meaning of America"—is languishing. A highly critical view of myth as the conservative, stabilizing element in culture has asserted itself;[52] and the subjectivist interests of a psychological history are challenged by the hard-edged externality of a sociological history. This breakaway from the stance of the postwar era has pro-duced some hopes for a "return to ideology," but they have borne little fruit.[53] The contemporary mood remains very largely anti-rationalist: more concerned with organizations than with beliefs, more responsive to experience than to ideas. Its principal contri-bution to the study of intellectual history may be to relieve that enterprise of over-extended commitments. Historians interested in how and what people think can now cultivate their rich and curious garden without assuming plenary responsiblity for explaining American history.

Insofar as intellectual history persists as a special field, it might do well to recall its traditional objectives and maintain them. Those aims overlap in manifold ways, and in the ideal case converge. Yet a single scholar can rarely do justice to all of them. Only the very greatest intellectual historians have accomplished the kind of total assessment that gives us the structure of a state of mind, its special value and attainments, and also its relation to events. An activist bias in the American historical profession has almost always played down the first and second objectives while magnifying the third. An appreciation of the variety of goals subsumed under the rubric "intellectual history" might liberate individual historians to develop more freely their own emphases and combinations. Man's heritage of thought and culture is too important and too complex to be studied only for its relevance to political or social behavior and otherwise left in the keeping of nonhistorical disciplines. At best, the latter have a highly circumscribed view of the past. Some of them have lost touch even with their own historical roots.

The label "intellectual history" has not only covered objectives that are hard to combine; it has also disguised wide differences in the level of inquiry. Pitched at one level, intellectual history deals chiefly with ideas; at another it deals chiefly with culture. Our nomenclature might better serve a desirable diversity if we retained more commonly the old distinction—inexact but useful, and dating back at least to the time of Buckle and Lecky—between the history of ideas and the history of culture or civilization. Under the influence of modern anthropology, "cultural history" has largely displaced "the history of civilization," a term that now seems too pretentious for application to any single country. Yet an essential difference between the type of book that Tyler and Parrington called the history of ideas and the type that Eggleston and Beard called the history of civilization persists. The history of ideas may be described as providing a relatively intensive analysis of clearly articulated ideas, whereas cultural history takes up a wider range of data in searching for the "style" or the unifying values of a group or a society.[54] One might say that in studying collective mentalities, cultural history looks for a configuration while the history of ideas seeks the cutting edge.

Neither, of course, should stand alone. As cultural history, the record of human consciousness has breadth and density, but tends to be static or repetitive. The history of ideas deals much more with individual initiative. There we see more clearly the emergence of innovation, the conflict between alternative choices. If the study of culture highlights structures, while the study of ideas (and events) brings movement and change to the fore, it is a great task of history to link one to the other, and so to catch the flux of patterns by the glint of their connecting threads. Still, scholars' inclinations vary widely. The difficulties at each level of inquiry are acute. Many might feel more comfortable and more definite about their own priorities if they had greater recourse to the distinction between cultural history and the history of ideas.

# 4

---

# THE REORIENTATION
# OF AMERICAN CULTURE
# IN THE 1890's

HERE IS MY FIRST, *preliminary effort to practice a kind of cultural history advocated in the preceding essay, namely the type that correlates diverse phenomena with the object of defining the spirit of an age. To be more exact, I have dealt here not with a single, undifferentiated age, but rather with the transition from one cultural system to another. I have sought thereby to suggest the character of each system by contrast with the other. Focusing on a phase of transition has the added merit of offsetting the static quality to which cultural history is prone. I am sensible of many shortcomings in the present essay, which I hope some day to correct in a more extended work. Nevertheless, the venture seemed worth making in view of a general neglect of this type of inquiry in American historiography.*

*This paper also points forward to the range of problems discussed in Part III below. Today's historians need to take account of two antithetical views of the American past. We need somehow to bring together a renewed appreciation of conflict in our history with the understanding of consensus which was so heavily stressed in the scholarship of the 1950's. One way of recognizing (I will not say harmonizing) both conflict and consensus is proposed in Chapter 8. Another way is illustrated in the present essay.*

*Consensus history gave primacy to the presumably enduring, distinctive unities of national character. The principal challenge to the national-character school has come—understandably enough—through the study of internal social antagonisms. Yet one should also conceive of national character as fluid and incomplete because of the intrusion of external forces. The present essay deals only with the latter. I have deliberately excluded from consideration the multiplicity of ethnic and regional sub-cultures that criss-crossed whatever unities America possessed. I have concentrated instead on the larger relations between American and European cultures. My object is not to trace specific influences but rather to observe a convergence between the spirit of a people and the spirit of an age. I have proceeded on the hypothesis that a national culture develops through an interplay between its own inherent tendencies and a wider set of influences and conditions, reaching across national lines, which affect a whole civilization more or less simultaneously. May it not be possible to clarify the successive phases of cultural history by counterposing the horizontal nexus of period character to the vertical thrust of national character?*

*A shorter version of this paper appeared in* The Origins of Modern Consciousness, *ed. John Weiss (Detroit: Wayne State University Press, 1965), 25–48; that portion of this article is used with the permission of the Wayne State University Press.*

## I

SOME YEARS AGO Professor Henry Steele Commager ventured the arresting hypothesis that the 1890's formed the "watershed of American history."[1] His argument attracted much notice, falling in as it did with a general pedagogical tendency to conceive of recent American history as beginning about that time. Many, however, remain unconvinced. If a truly fundamental alteration in the course of things occurred around the end of the nineteenth century, in what experience did it center? No single event, such as a major war or a drastic social upheaval, offered an obvious answer. By surveying a varied and miscellaneous array of items, Professor Commager depicted a multitude of particular transitions rather than an integral change; the decade looked more like a concourse than a watershed. In some respects it was not a decade at all. In considering intellectual movements Professor Commager ranged across a much longer span of time and emphasized innovations in political, religious, and scientific thinking that can be located perhaps more exactly in the seventies and eighties than in the nineties.

After Commager's study appeared, the whole notion of searching out basic discontinuities in the course of American history fell for a time into some discredit. Professor Cunliffe, for example, suggested that American historians strain to find watersheds because their own history has flowed so smoothly and continuously forward.[2] Yet history, as a coherent body of knowledge, cannot do very well without some principle of periodization that takes advantage of changes in tempo and direction. If we dispense with the metaphor of watersheds and flatten the concept of revolution, we will perforce fall back before long on such good old standbys as the turning-point and the crisis. It is therefore instructive for students of American history to observe that leading authorities on European intellectual history have been discovering a major crisis or turning-point at the end of the nineteenth century, and discovering it just when Americans seem most inclined to deny any comparable transformation on this side of the Atlantic.[3] If European culture was indeed undergoing a great upheaval, we have here an admirable opportunity for testing the vaunted continuity of American culture. Assuming that momentous changes were occurring in Europe, how much did Americans participate in them?

The question might be formulated in different ways. It would be possible to choose certain major events or institutions of the late nineteenth century, such as the rise of imperialism or the growth of bureaucracy, and ask how Americans responded or contributed. Alternatively, one might examine in depth one or more major ideas as they emerged in a European and in an American setting, ideas such as socialism or liberalism, or the images and feelings imbedded in an international art movement like Art Nouveau. A third approach is that of the cultural historian. His perspective cannot afford to exclude the other two. He cannot ignore the substantial instruments of power that concern the institutional historian; he cannot overlook the developed systems of thought that occupy the historian of ideas. But his special interest centers on the configurations of attitude and habit that connect these different levels of experience at a given point in time.

Although cultural history seeks a unifying vision, it cannot do everything. It does not lend itself very well to locating the source of change. It lacks the specificity—it does not have the narrative thrust —that enables us to follow a path of sequential activity and call it cause and effect. Cultural history also tends to sacrifice some of the delicacy and precision that distinguish the history of ideas at its best. The cultural historian's delineation of characteristic or pervasive modes of experience prevents him from doing full justice to the singular quality or complexity of any one perception of the world. On the other hand, cultural history excels in indicating the range or scope of historical phenomena. It comes into play in an effort to draw the outlines of national character or to define the spirit of an age. Its utility for coping with problems of periodization is unmatched; for historians, in order to distinguish one era from another, must either arbitrarily assign a preponderating influence of one level of experience, such as economics or foreign policy, or they must discern an underlying shift in the cultural pattern.

If such a shift got under way about the end of the nineteenth century, it was manifest then only in an emergent and formative stage. One must look for a set of attitudes that became prominent at that time but developed much more fully in the twentieth century. Phenomena unique to a particular decade can easily mislead the cultural historian in search of underlying trends. The nineties were —as every student knows—an unusually troubled decade, memorable as a time of economic crisis, industrial strife, and ethnic turmoil. It would be well, however, to put aside for the moment our usual preoccupation with angry Populists and striking workers, in order to detect in the broad reaches of middle-class life less dramatic but more enduring symptoms of cultural change. There one is struck by the appearance of a temper of mind that may also illuminate the rhetoric of agrarian and proletarian unrest, if not its substance.

Our inquiry may begin on the campuses of American colleges and universities. The great reconstruction of American higher education had already occurred in the 1870's and '80's. In the nineties the structure of the modern university solidified. Within that structure, however, the life of the undergraduate now acquired its own glamor and took on a significance quite distinct from the official goals of the institution. The twentieth century was to put a special premium on youth, a period of life that became differentiated from the dependence of childhood on one side and from the sober responsibilities of later adulthood on the other; and it was in a college setting about the end of the nineteenth century that the model of a youth culture came into being.[4] Clark University's President, G. Stanley Hall, published in 1904 an epochal study, *Adolescence,* summing up ideas he had been formulating since the 1880's, which gave the sanction of academic psychology to a phase of life supposedly characterized by a maximum of spontaneity, freedom, and vital energy. But already the avid fans of Frank Merriwell knew something of what Hall was writing about. Invented by a pulp magazine writer in 1896, Merriwell, the carefree champion of every sport at Yale, was the first great hero of American popular culture whose exploits took place on a college playing field.[5]

## II

In 1894 a group of Dartmouth alumni asked Richard Hovey, a young and dedicated poet, to write a new college song for his alma mater. Dartmouth's heritage of Puritan piety had faded; its rural isolation no longer seemed an asset; the school needed a fresh, up-to-date public image. This Hovey obligingly supplied in the rousingly successful "Men of Dartmouth":

> They have the still North in their hearts,
> The hill-winds in their veins,
> And the granite of New Hampshire
> In their muscles and their brains.[6]

This chilly, rockbound portrait, naïve as it may sound today in its unconscious anti-intellectualism, exactly suited the emerging, collegiate spirit of the nineties. Hovey's song not only subordinated mind to muscle; it also associated both of these with the ruggedness of nature rather than the refinements of culture. In doing so, it turned the disadvantage of Dartmouth's location into an asset: it suggested to the men of Dartmouth their particular claim to the virility that College men throughout the country eagerly desired.

A rage for competitive athletics and for outdoor activities of all kinds was sweeping the campuses of the nation. A combative team spirit became virtually synonymous with college spirit; and athletic prowess became a major determinant of institutional status. Football made the greatest impact. Sedulously cultivated by Yale in the 1880's, it expanded into a big business after Walter Camp in 1889 named the first All-American team. While football dominated the autumn, older sports such as baseball and track flourished in the spring. To fill the winter gap and to arrest the flight of students from the confines of the gymnasium, a YMCA teacher invented basketball in 1891. It was taken up almost at once. Intercollegiate wrestling matches soon followed.[7] Dartmouth, following Hovey's lead, learned to feature skiing and winter carnivals.

The transformation of the colleges into theaters of organized physical combat illustrates a master impulse that seized the American people in the 1890's and reshaped their history in the ensuing decades. Theodore Roosevelt articulated that impulse in a famous speech delivered in 1899, "The Strenuous Life." Denouncing "the soft spirit of the cloistered life" and "the base spirit of gain," Roosevelt told his listeners to "boldly face the life of strife . . . for it is only through strife, through hard and dangerous endeavor, that we shall ultimately win the goal of true national greatness."[8] If these words struck the keynote of Roosevelt's own career, they also sounded the tocsin of a new era. Countless others, in their various ways, expressed similar feelings. John Jay Chapman, a leading cultural critic, flayed the tepid conformity, the pervasive desire to please, the shuffling and circumspection, the "lack of passion in the American." Even Henry James—though in most respects he was a paragon of the older culture that valued restraint—put into the mouths of his emotionally starved protagonists a choked cry for vivifying experience. "Don't forget that you're young," Strether tells little Bilham in *The Ambassadors*. "Live all you can; it's a mistake not to. It doesn't so much matter what you do in particular, so long as you have your life."[9] Common folk felt much the same way. A whole range of newly minted epithets gained currency in the 1890's: sissy, pussyfoot, cold feet, stuffed shirt.[10] All of these bespoke an impatience with the more civilized vices, the vices of gentility.

From the middle of the nineteenth century until about 1890 Americans on the whole had submitted docilely enough to the gathering restrictions of a highly industrialized society. They learned to live in cities, to sit in rooms cluttered with bric-a-brac, to limit the size of their families, to accept the authority of professional elites, to mask their aggressions behind a thickening façade of respectability, and to comfort themselves with a faith in automatic material progress. Above all, Americans learned to conform to the discipline of machinery. The time clock, introduced into offices and factories in the early 1890's, signaled an advanced stage in the mechanization of life.[11]

By that time, a profound spiritual reaction was developing. It took many forms, but it was everywhere a hunger to break out of the frustrations, the routine, and the sheer dullness of an urban-industrial culture. It was everywhere an urge to be young, masculine, and adventurous. In the 1890's the new, activist mood was only beginning to challenge the restraint and decorum of the "Gilded Age." Only after 1897, when the oppressive weight of a long, grim economic depression lifted, did a demand for vivid and masterful experience dominate American politics. Yet the dynamism that characterized the whole political and social scene from the turn of the century through World War I emerged during the 1890's in large areas of popular culture. To some of these areas historians have not yet paid enough attention to appreciate the extent and nature of the change that was occurring. We are well aware of the aggressive nationalism that sprang up after 1890. We do not so often notice analogous ferments in other spheres: a boom in sports and recreation; a revitalized interest in untamed nature; a quickening of popular music; an unsettling of the condition of women.

The sports revolution in the colleges was part of a much broader upsurge of enthusiasm for outdoor recreation and physical culture in the American public at large. The growing zest for both spectator and participant sports amazed contemporary observers in the early nineties. The most universal sport was bicycling, one of the great crazes of the decade. Primarily social and recreational rather than a means of necessary transportation, bicycles reached a total of one million in 1893, ten million in 1900. Bicycle clubs and championship races excited enormous interest. Among games, baseball retained its primacy at both the professional and sandlot levels.[12] It did not, however, enjoy the sensational growth of other sports that catered more directly to a taste for speed or a taste for violence. Racing of various kinds, to say nothing of basketball, satisfied one; football and boxing fulfilled the other. Only boxing, among the spectacles of the nineties, grew as rapidly as football in public appeal. Most states of the union still outlawed professional prize-fighting as a relic of barbarism. Nevertheless, it began to lose its unsavory reputation after 1892, when padded gloves replaced bare fists and "Gentleman Jim" Corbett displayed an artful technique in defeating John L. Sullivan.[13] Henceforth heavyweight champions loomed large among American folk heroes.

An accompanying gospel of health through rugged exercise spread literally by leaps and bounds. Of the many shamans who arose to lead the cult, Bernarr Macfadden was the most successful. His carrer began at the World's Fair in Chicago in 1893, where he demonstrated the muscular attractions of an exerciser. He advanced through health clubs and lectures and won a national audience as publisher of the magazine *Physical Culture*. The first issue, appearing in 1899, flaunted his slogan: "Weakness Is a Crime."[14]

Closely linked with the boom in sports and health came an enthusiasm for the tonic freshness and openness of nature. This too had both a participant and a spectatorial aspect. At its mildest, participation meant escaping to the country astride a bicycle, taking up the newly imported game of golf, or going to the innumerable vacation resorts that emphasized their outdoor facilities. Somewhat more strenuously, it meant hiking and camping. In 1889 nature-lovers launched a campaign in behalf of California's redwood forests, and the following year Congress created Yosemite, Sequoia, and General Grant National Parks. Here was the beginning of a sustained movement to preserve the American wilderness from the encroachments of civilization. During the ensuing decade hundreds of nature-study clubs formed to encourage amateur naturalists. At least fifty-two periodicals devoted to wild life began publication.[15] In fact, the flood of nature writing, based on intimate knowledge and vivid observation, registered a major shift in popular interests. Only the leading novelists exceeded the popularity of some of the nature writers, such as John Muir and Ernest Thompson Seton, whose first books appeared in 1894 and 1898 respectively.[16]

Although the outdoor movement clearly drew upon a traditional American distrust of the city, it also ministered to the more general psychological discontents of the 1890's. Among the values that middle-class Americans were rediscovering in nature, two stand out. For one, the great outdoors signified spaciousness—an imaginative release from the institutional restraints and confinements Americans had accepted since the Civil War. It is suggestive that one of the features of the return to nature was a passion for bird-watching. In a six-year-period New York and Boston publishers sold more than 70,000 textbooks on birds, while a children's magazine, *Birds,* reached a circulation of 40,000 in its first year of publication.[17] Congress had chosen a great soaring bird as the national emblem over a century before, and a bird on the wing continued to symbolize for Americans the boundless space they wished to inhabit.

Secondly, nature meant—as Hovey's description of Dartmouth men indicated—virility. It represented that masculine hardiness and power that suddenly seemed an absolutely indispensable remedy for the artificiality and effeteness of late nineteenth-century urban life. Nothing revealed the craving for nature's untamed strength so well as the best-selling fiction of the late nineties. For decades the popular novel had concentrated on domestic or rococo subjects rather than wilderness adventures. Above the level of the dime novel, the wild

West had played very little part in fiction since the 1850's. Now it came back with a rush in a best-selling Canadian thriller, Ralph Connor's *Black Rock* (1898), in Jack London's red-blooded stories of the Klondike, and in Owen Wister's classic cowboy tale, *The Virginian* (1902). In effect, these and other writers were answering James Lane Allen's plea of 1897 for a reassertion of the masculine principle of virility and instinctive action in a literature too much dominated by the feminine principle of refinement and delicacy.[18]

A similarly muscular spirit invaded popular verse and music. The conventional style of song in the late nineteenth century was mournful and nostalgic. It projected a life heavy with disappointment and regrets, a life girt with limitations, a life drenched in tears. The fascination with death in such poems as Eugene Field's "Little Boy Blue," and with parting in such hit tunes as "After the Ball," betrayed a loss of youthfulness of American popular culture. Against this drowsy mood, a new generation of high-spirited poets and musicians affirmed the masculine principle. Richard Hovey won a great popular success as co-author of *Songs from Vagabondia* (1894), which perfectly expressed the fresh out-of-doors spirit. Like no poems since Whitman's, these combined the love of nature, the freedom of the open road, the rollicking comradeship of men, and the tang of vivid experience.[19]

Meanwhile, cheerful energetic tunes spread from the midways and outdoor amusement parks that were themselves symptoms of a new era. "Ta-ra-ra-boom-der-e," first published in 1891, struck a new, rhythmically vital note. Thereafter itinerant Negro pianists taught the white public the excitement of ragtime, a form of syncopation applied against a steady bass rhythm. A high-kicking dance step called the cakewalk spread along with the ragtime craze. In vain, custodians of respectability denounced this "nigger music" and the "vulgar," "filthy" prancing that went with it.[20]

Both the new music and the new athleticism were connected with the emergence of the New Woman. Her salient traits were boldness and radiant vigor. She shed the Victorian languor that had turned American middle-class society—as William Dean Howells noted in 1872—into a hospital for invalid females. Women took to the open road in tremendous numbers on bicycles suitably altered by an American inventer. They sat for portraits clutching tennis rackets; they might be seen at the new golf clubs or at the race tracks smoking cigarettes. In 1901 they could learn from Bernarr Macfadden's book, *The Power and Beauty of Superb Womanhood,* that vigorous exercise "will enable a woman to develop in every instance muscular strength almost to an equal degree with man."[21]

> Running, jumping, and natation, navigation, ambulation—
> So she seeks for recreation in a whirl.
> She's a highly energetic, undissuadable, magnetic,
> Peripatetic, athletic kind of girl![22]

The New Woman was masculine also in her demand for political power. The women's suffrage movement had been crotchety and unpopular; now it blossomed into a great nationwide middle-class force.[23]

While women became more manly, men became more martial. By 1890 the sorrow and weariness left by the Civil War had passed; jingoism and a deliberate cultivation of the military virtues ensued. The United States picked quarrels with Italy, Chile, and Great Britain before it found a satisfactory target in the liberation of Cuba. A steady build-up of naval power accompanied these crises. The rising respect for military prowess also manifested itself in a remarkable cult of Napoleon. The first two installments of Ida Tarbell's biography of Napoleon in *McClure's Magazine* doubled its paid circulation; and hers was only one of twenty-eight books about the Corsican general published in the United States in the three years from 1894 to 1896. For a collective symbol of the strenuous life, myth-makers depended heavily on the Anglo-Saxon "race," which they endowed with unprecedented ferocity. A Kansas senator, for example, proudly described his "race" as "the most arrogant and rapacious, the most exclusive and indomitable in history."[24]

Meanwhile, flag ceremonies, such as the newly-contrived pledge of allegiance, entered the school houses of the land. Patriotic societies multiplied as never before. In function they resembled the cheer leaders who were becoming so prominent a part of the big football spectacles and who lifted the massed ranks of students into a collective glory. The link between the new athleticism and the new jingoism was especially evident in the yellow press: William Randolph Hearst's *New York Journal* created the modern sports page in 1896, just when its front page filled with atrocity stories of the bloody debauchery of Spanish brutes in Cuba.[25] At the same time the new music produced such martial airs as John Philip Sousa's masterpiece of patriotic fervor, "Stars and Stripes Forever" (1897), and "A Hot Time in the Old Town" (1896), which Theodore Roosevelt adopted as the official song of his Rough Riders. Indeed, Roosevelt was the outstanding fugleman of the whole gladiatorial spirit. He loved the great outdoors, the challenge of sports, the zest of political combat, the danger of war. He exhorted women to greater fecundity. He brought boxing into the White House and contributed immensely to its respectability.[26]

The change in temper I have been describing did not occur in the United States alone. It swept over much of western Europe about the same time. Its most obvious manifestations appeared in the navalism and jingoism of the time: the various national defense societies, the Pan-German League, the bombast of William II, the sensational journalism of the Harmsworth brothers, the emotions that swirled around General Boulanger and Captain Dreyfus. Europe was more receptive than America to the militaristic aspects of the new mood. Two Englishmen, H. Rider Haggard and Rudyard Kipling, popularized the material and masculine adventure story before respectable American authors turned to that genre; and the Americans did not insist, as did Kipling and the German youth movement, on the values of discipline and obedience. In other respects, however, America may have some claim to priority and leadership. The outdoors movement may have started in America, although England and Germany were not far behind.[27] The New Woman, together with her bicycle, materialized in England and in America about the same time. Demands for a freer sexual morality got an earlier hearing in England, but the achievement of political rights and economic independence came more easily in this country than anywhere in Europe. The very phrase "New Woman" may have originated in the talk of an American character in an English novel that had its greatest success in the United States. Sarah Grand's *The Heavenly Twins,* published in 1893, expounded feminist ideas in a glamorous setting and sold five times as many copies in America as in England. [28]

In the sports revival, which also affected both continents, Americans seized a commanding lead. No people except the British loved athletic contests so much; and the Americans clearly excelled in ferocity. They won most of the events in the early Olympic Games, nine out of fourteen at Athens in 1896 and fourteen out of twenty at Paris in 1900. They racked up a disproportionate number of "world records."[29] They so dominated professional boxing that the championship of the United States became, from 1892 onward, identical with that of the world. A French observer, bemused by the American taste for pugilism, concluded that it was "too brutal a sight for a Frenchman of the nineteenth century."[30]

On the other hand, Europeans found the energy of American music much to their liking. "Ta-ra-ra-boom-der-e" spread through Britain and beyond like an epidemic. "No other song ever took a people in quite the same way," an English historian tells us. "It would seem to have been the absurd *ça ira* of a generation bent upon kicking over the traces."[31] Translated into French as "Tha-mara-buom-di-hé," the song proved a great hit in the leading Parisian cabarets. Across the Atlantic also went the cakewalk, dazzling the music halls of London and Paris, and Sousa's band, giving Europe its first taste of ragtime.[32] The taste suited. In 1908 Claude Debussy used this American idiom for *The Golliwog's Cakewalk*. Altogether, the United States exercised initiative only within some aspects of the burgeoning activism of the 1890's and was not deeply involved in its most sinister implications. Nevertheless, American influences were widely felt. Europeans who feared the threat the new spirit posed to traditional values sometimes called it Americanism.[33]

To say that Americans took part in a farreaching reaction against the constrictions of a routinized society does not, of course, explain why the reaction occurred. Historians have no satisfactory answer to such large problems. Recognition that we are dealing with an international movement—with a change of phase evident throughout the western world—makes quixotic any effort to explain the change in its American context alone. Yet the mentality I have been describing did have undeniable American roots. Not wholly new, it was to some extent the reawakening of a spirit present in American life virtually from the beginning. Since the Antinomian outbreak that Anne Hutchinson led in 1636, an exuberant libertarian aggressiveness, impatient of restraint and tradition, had ebbed and flowed in America. It reached a crest in the transcendental ecstacies of Emerson, Garrison, and Whitman and was then submerged during the Civil War and the decades that followed.

Some evidence for suspecting that the strenuous life in the late nineteenth century was partly a revival of buried impulses emerges in its rhetoric. Apostles of strenuosity repeatedly lamented the excessive refinement and the enervating tendencies of modern civilization; they saw themselves as revitalizing primitive virtues. Sports enthusiasts declared that "this vaunted age" needed "a saving touch of honest, old-fashioned barbarism, that when we come to die, we shall die leaving men behind us, and not a race of eminently respectable female saints."[34] Imperialists warned of the exhaustion that might overtake an effete society, confined within fixed geographical limits; they called for a resumption of the vigorous outward push of the frontier. The chief ideologists for the New Woman harked back to a primitive era of strong females, before men enslaved them in the home.[35] In many such instances the activists' rhetoric affirmed a continuity with an older, pre-modern culture.

It is possible to locate the social sources of the continuity to some extent. The new élan of the nineties sought particularly to loosen the constraints and conformities binding urban, middle-class life. This activism had a base in other groups who had never submitted completely to Victorian gentility because they were outside its range. Activists were impatient with what one of them described as "the bourgeois spirit [of] that element which dares not use slang, shrinks from audacity, rarely utters a bold sentiment and as rarely feels one. It is as correct as Sunday clothes and as innocuous as sterilized milk, *but it is not aristocratic.*"[36] Nor was it plebeian. The strenuous life invoked values that had persisted both above and below the great American middle class. Each of the manifestations of the new activism that I have described thus far was already a part of patrician experience on the one hand and of the life of the poor on the other.

Consider, for instance, the sports revolution and the accompanying return to nature. Rough outdoor sports were habitual pleasures of rural gentry and small town loafers before they became respectable in the cities. Bloody, bare-knuckled prize-fighting gladdened the hearts of miners, saloon-keepers, and their rowdy patrons throughout the decades of civic opprobrium, while the "science of boxing" according to the Queensberry rules first took hold in elite athletic clubs. Baseball too was initially played by gentlemen's clubs like the Knickerbockers in New York; football originated as an ivy-college sport.[37] The open spaces of the West always appealed, of course, to the pioneer type. Moreover, the western adventure story enjoyed a continuous vogue among the uncultivated readers of the dime novel during the era when respectable publishers concentrated on the idylls of domesticity.

Other strands in the activism of the nineties also combined patrician with plebeian life-styles and brought them to bear on middle-class culture. The novelty of the New Woman was in part her middle-class status. The daughters of the poor had never been immobilized within a strictly domestic existence, and such patrician ladies as Josephine Shaw Lowell and Julia Ward Howe had enjoyed a wide sphere of authority during the post-Civil War decades. Rag-time music evolved from the vigorous folk melodies of the black peasantry of the Deep South; and among its early supporters were Society leaders in Chicago, New York, and Newport.[38] Finally, the belligerent nationalism of the nineties can be traced back to a persistent jingoism among the underprivileged masses, aided by an imperialist elite. Both groups despised the timidity of what Roosevelt called "the moneyed and semi-cultivated classes."[39] In short, the new vitality may be understood as an infusion of lower-class and upper-class aggressiveness into the middle-class world.

Still, it was in some sense a new phase in American cultural history that was coming into being, not a mere revival of pre-Victorian values. Even as a movement of revitalization, the activism of the nineties received from its context a character very different from the early American ebullience. *That* had flowered in a time when many traditional institutions were losing authority; the outward reach into open space was a common fact as well as an ideal. *This* was occurring within the confines of an increasingly organized society.[40] The steady growth of rational structures, making for an ever more integrated, impersonal way of life, was irreversible. The new activism could do little more than reform those structures or cultivate the life of impulse within them. Consequently, the emergent culture of the Strenuous Age had an ambiguous relation to its institutional matrix. In some measure a rebellion against the constraints of a highly organized society, it was also an accommodation to those constraints, a way of coming to terms with them.

## III

The degree of innovation that a cultural change releases appears more clearly if we look not just at the thrust of mass movements but also at what the most creative minds were doing. It remains, therefore, to ask if American intellectuals underwent an awakening comparable to the upheaval in popular feelings. How much were intellectuals involved in the psychic turbulence of the 1890's? The Americans did not unleash as direct an assault on genteel culture as some of their European contemporaries mounted. Yet a change of mood among intellectuals on both continents paralleled the shift in middle-class attitudes.

The reorientation among intellectuals followed upon the dominion that a materialistic outlook had won during the immediately preceding decades. From the 1860's through the 1880's, in Europe and America alike, the combined prestige of science and business enterprise shaped the direction of thought. During these years romantic idealism declined. So did religious vitality in the face of a sweeping secularization of values. Ornateness and a certain heaviness of style prevailed. All encompassing, monistic systems of thought were in favor: Spencerian and Hegelian systems contended in America; Comtean positivism and Marxian socialism loomed large in Europe. A triumphant belief in evolutionary progress, although much stronger in America than in Europe, everywhere blunted moral sensitivity.

By 1890 this vesture of assurance and complacency was wearing through. It failed to cover the emotional and material needs of the laboring classes; it did not entirely smother the conscience of the middle class; and it was too tight a fit for many intellectuals. For the latter, the cult of progress, stability, and materialism was becoming oppressive and suffocating. It brought restraint and uniformity into the world of thought without resolving the increasing conflicts in society.

The first response of intellectuals to the obvious social dislocations of an urban, industrial age was an attempt to strengthen the framework of order and to reinterpret the path of progress. The equipment of liberalism with a collective social ethic constituted the principal achievement of social thought both in England and in America in the 1880's—a work accomplished in one by Thomas Hill Green and the Fabians, and in the other by Henry George, Lester F. Ward, William Dean Howells, and a variety of historical economists. But these ideas made only modest headway in the following decade, while the problems they addressed grew much more acute. The special significance of the 1890's lay in a change of mood that swept many intellectuals beyond the earnest sobriety of the seventies and eighties. A readjustment of rational principles in the light of existing facts seemed in itself ineffective and uninteresting.

Two other strategies were possible; and the clash between them pervaded intellectual life. One might, in contempt or despair, spurn the trust in progress and find solace in contemplating the decline of a moribund civilization. Or one might look beyond the conventional framework of thought for access to fresh sources of energy. The first alternative was the counsel of defeat; the second was a call to liberation. One way led to pessimism, decadence, and withdrawal into art for art's sake. The other pointed to a heightened activity and an exuberant sense of power. Both alternatives broke sharply with the complacent faith in material progress and human rationality that had ruled the Western world for two generations. Both the pessimists and the activists of the 1890's felt that the rational schemata of their time had become closed systems, imprisoning the human spirit. Pessimists accepted the denial of responsibility and purpose. Activists, on the other hand, attacked closed systems and created meanings from the flux of experience.

The acid of defeat and the elixir of liberation mingled in the intellectual ferment of the decade. A good many Americans as well as Europeans tasted both, with lasting effect. In general, however, one may say that the elixir proved an effective antidote to the acid. The strenuous spirit so prominent in popular culture quite generally overcame a defeatist spirit among intellectuals. The melancholy of the *fin-de-siècle* belied its name: it lifted before the end of the century.

This was especially the case in the United States, where a pessimistic outlook had only recently taken root in a serious way. Worldly pessimism comprised an important strain in European thought since the Enlightenment. Americans, however, had derived their sense of evil from the bracing doctrines of Calvinism, and they encountered the world with determination to resist it. Neither the terrors of personal frustration as in Poe nor the transcendental doubts of Melville had resulted in a pessimistic philosophy of life. The emergence of such an outlook was therefore a milestone in American intellectual history.

The melancholy and the ennui that invaded certain fastidious American minds in the late eighties and early nineties bore the direct imprint of European decadence. Schopenhauer together with Spinoza and Lucretius provided the basic philosophical structure for most of the poetry that George Santayana wrote in the nineties. Leopardi, Swinburne, and the English aesthetes supplied additional models for the circle of Harvard poets that formed around Santayana in those years. In New York Edgar Saltus, who also began from Schopenhauer, published delicately scandalous novels resembling those of Oscar Wilde in their knowing insolence and perverse wit. Others were reading Ernest Renan appreciatively. Renan instructed Henry Adams in the artistic uses of a spiritually exhausted religion, as Adams drifted from the South Seas to the cathedrals of France.[41] The same lesson reached a wide public through Harold Frederic's best-selling novel, *The Damnation of Theron Ware* (1896). Here an ultra-civilized, skeptical Catholic priest reveals to a simple-minded Methodist clergyman the world-weary elegance of a religion of art. "The truth is always relative, Mr. Ware," Father Forbes concludes.[42]

Other writers, untouched by European aestheticism, arrived at a grimmer sort of pessimism. There was, for example, the savage irony of the San Francisco journalist, Ambrose Bierce, whose first book of short stories, *Tales of Soldiers and Civilians* (1891), depicted a pointless, mocking destiny. There was Henry Adams' brother, Brooks, whose *Law of Civilization and Decay* (1895) diagnosed the decline of Western civilization since the defeat of Napoleon and its impending dissolution. This powerful, serious book was perhaps the first modern formulation of a cyclical theory of history. It was certainly the first full length American critique of the conception of history as progress. More informally, Mark Twain was reaching the same conclusion. His laughter turned increasingly into bitterness, visions of destruction welled up at the end of *A Connecticut Yankee* (1889), and by the late nineties an explicit fatalism convinced Twain that history was an endless cycle of cruelty and corruption, "a barren and meaningless process."[43] E. L. Godkin too was giving up hope for the future of American civilization. The toughest minded of all of the nation's social philosophers, William Graham Sumner, was warning his fellow countrymen that the utmost they could do was "to note and record their course as they are carried along" in the great stream of time.[44]

Such attitudes exemplified the naturalistic determinism that originated with Darwin and Spencer and became increasingly oppressive as the century waned. Until the 1890's American intellectuals had tempered the naturalistic creed with a supreme confidence in their own destiny. In Europe evolutionary thought slipped more easily into a dark vision of a blind and purposeless universe. Thus the naturalistic novel, in which man appears as the hapless plaything of great impersonal forces, was well established in France and England before Stephen Crane in 1893 published *Maggie,* the first American example of the genre. Pessimism seems to have invaded American minds only after the actual course of social change clearly refuted the liberating significance Americans had imputed to the evolutionary process. By 1890 the consolidation of big organizations, the massing of population, and the growing intensity of class conflict were inescapably apparent. These trends did not at all correspond to the individualizing movement that Herbert Spencer had confidently envisioned. Instead of an inevitable development from an "incoherent homogeneity to a definite, coherent heterogeneity," Brooks Adams observed a steady centralization and a loss of vital energy, which would result in anarchy. Henry refined the theory into one of a general degradation and dispersion of energy.[45] Many felt an erosion of their own independent station in society. Clearly, the survival of the fittest was not synonymous, as Darwinians formerly supposed, with the survival of the best. Nor did the course of events conform to the ancient belief in America's uniqueness, confidence in which had always provided an ultimate bulwark of the national faith in progress. "We are the first Americans," Woodrow Wilson gravely warned, "to entertain any serious doubts about the superiority of our own institutions as compared with the systems of Europe."[46]

A signal indication of the intensity of concern over these defeatist attitudes was the feverish discussion provoked by Max Nordau's book, *Degeneration.* I believe that no other European book of any kind published during the entire decade aroused so much comment in the American press. Even before its translation into English in 1895, the book received a long review in *The Critic.*[47] Soon the Sunday supplements and the daily papers were trumpeting its charges. Much of this attention resulted from the sheer sensationalism of Nordau's argument that the eminent artists and writers of the day were suffering from mental deterioration. Many, perhaps most, commentators regarded Nordau as at least as degenerate as the people he attacked. But his fundamental charge that the age was suffering from "a compound of feverish restlessness and blunted discouragement, of . . . vague qualms of a Dusk of Nations" touched a sensitive nerve.

When all this is said, the fact remains that pessimism became in America neither general nor profound. Sourness and irony Americans could sometimes stomach; they had little taste for despair. Even Henry Adams never ceased to struggle against despair, and Santayana transmuted it into a flawless serenity. Most American intellectuals resisted pessimism. Philosophers (with the partial exception of Santayana) rallied against it; literary critics denounced it; social scientists were challenged rather than overcome by it. Accordingly, the voices of negation rose from rather special quarters: from people who were being left behind. The most somber temperaments belonged, on the one hand, to old men like Twain and Sumner, who had fought the good fight through the seventies and eighties and who now lost heart; or they belonged, on the other hand, to men of patrician background like Adams, Saltus, and the Harvard poets, scions of old and cultivated families who felt displaced in a pushing, competitive, bourgeois world.

The naturalistic novelists cannot be included among either the old men or the patricians. They were young, and they came from middle-class homes. But it requires no close inspection to discover that Norris, Crane, London, and even Dreiser were only partly fatalistic. Unlike many European naturalists, they expressed the affirmative as well as the negative possibilities of their age. The American naturalists gloried in identifying themselves with the triumphant strength of nature or with the struggles of embattled man. Instead of observing life clinically, they celebrated power. "The world," intoned Frank Norris, "wants men, great, strong, harsh, brutal men—men with purpose who let nothing, nothing, nothing stand in their way."[48] Dreiser and London shared Norris's fascination with the ruthless pursuit of success. Crane spent his volatile life imagining and seeking war. Here, as Van Wyck Brooks has pointed out, began the cave-man tendency in modern American literature.[49] In the fierce joy of conflict these writers discovered the activist reply to the spectre of an indifferent universe.

No one better reveals the instability of the pessimism of the nineties than its most systematic exponent, Brooks Adams. Younger and less cosmopolitan than his brother Henry, who remained generally defeatist, Brooks underwent a great conversion around 1898. He decided that the Spanish-American War disproved his theory of history. Evidently centralization was leading not to a degradation but to a revival of national energy. Only Europe, not America, is decaying, Brooks chortled. "I am for the new world—the new America, the new empire . . . we are the people of destiny."[50] And he became henceforth an activist, who bombarded his fellow countrymen with advice on geopolitical strategy and public administration.

Thus Brooks Adams illustrates two of the spheres in which the strenuous life came to intellectual fruition. The escape from pessimism flung him into reform as well as imperialism. Since imperialism proved after a short while an unattractive outlet for American effort, his attention turned increasingly in the early twentieth century to the uses of power in domestic affairs. This happened to a great many American intellectuals. We know that imperialism and progressivism were closely related crusades, and it seems clear that together they largely banish gloom and anxiety in favor of an optimistic, adventurous engagement in social change.[51] The activism of the nineties contributed, therefore, to the hearty interest that progressive intellectuals showed in *doing* things, in closing with immediate practical realities, in concentrating on techniques rather than sweeping theories. The early twentieth century was not a very congenial period in America for the speculative thinker with interests remote from the facts of contemporary life. It was a time of administrative energy and functional thought.

Must we then conclude that the new activism was generally anti-intellectual and had little constructive impact on other areas of thought, beyond concrete social issues? Were its positive achievements only visceral and practical? Or did the shattering of closed systems and the relief of pessimism also enlarge the imaginative resources of American intellectuals? These questions do not admit of any final answer. But a brief comparison of three major intellectuals who participated in the cultural revolution of the 1890's may suggest how stimulating it could be in very diverse fields.[52]

## IV

William James was neither the first of the American pragmatists nor in every respect the greatest, but he was surely the most passionately concerned with emancipating his fellow men from tradition, apathy, and routine. His predecessor Charles S. Peirce was preoccupied with traditional metaphysical and logical problems, his successor John Dewey with gaining rational control of experience. James, standing between them, was the arch-foe of all intellectual systems, less concerned with organizing thought or experience than with validating their manifold possibilities. Although each of the major pragmatists took part in the intellectual life of the 1890's, James belongs to that decade in a very special sense. Having anticipated much earlier its revolt against pessimism and fatalism, James applied himself intensively to its spiritual needs. His *Principles of Psychology* came out in 1890. Thereafter he grew beyond his first career as a psychologist, greatly enlarged his interests and sympathies, and launched pragmatism as a broad philosophical movement.

For James the nineties were years of fulfillment and fame. For two young men born in the 1860's—Frederick Jackson Turner and Frank Lloyd Wright—this was the crucially formative period, when the emancipation that James preached was taking effect. Turner received his Ph.D. at Johns Hopkins in 1890 and returned to Wisconsin to work out his own ideas about American history. In the next few years all of his major ideas emerged. The famous address of 1893 on the significance of the frontier announced his revolt against the eastern, European-oriented view of American history that then prevailed. In other work of the mid-nineties, Turner inaugurated a broadly economic interpretation of American history in terms of sectional cleavages.[53] Wright, a budding Chicago architect, also declared independence in 1893 by quitting his beloved master, Louis Sullivan, and opening his own office. During the course of the decade Wright developed his own personal, flexible style in opposition both to Sullivan's sentimentality and to the conventions of the European architectural tradition. Unknown to one another, James, Turner, and Wright were the great leavening and liberating figures in their respective disciplines at the turn of the century.

None of them engaged in the crude, swaggering bombast so prevalent in the popular activism of the period. Indeed, James roundly attacked people like Theodore Roosevelt who were arousing "the aboriginal capacity for murderous excitement which lies sleeping" in every bosom, and he once coolly remarked of his friend Oliver Wendell Holmes, Jr., that "Mere excitement is an immature ideal, unworthy of the Supreme Court's official endorsement."[54] Nevertheless, James, Wright, and Turner were in their own ways hardy, fighting men, full of zest for new experience, in love with novelty and experiment, eager to adapt philosophy, architecture, and history to the ever-changing needs of the present hour. James himself struck the distinctive note of the 1890's by interpreting all ideas as plans for action and by exalting the will.

All three men possessed exuberant, optimistic, restless personalities. Their brimming energies threatened continually to overflow any imposed discipline, so much so in the cases of James and Turner that neither succeeded in finishing the big, systematic book he wished to write. Neither in his intellectual habits was at all methodical. "Turner bubbled it out," one of his students remembers,[55] and the same could equally have been said of James. Wright had the strongest personality of the three. He ran away from home, scorned all formal education, and built within himself an oracular self-confidence touched with arrogance.[56] Only Wright wore his hair long to flaunt his independence, but James and Turner also enjoyed a poetic flair and a lilting heart.

Intellectually, their deepest affinity arose from a common opposition to all closed and static patterns of order. James's repugnance for a "block universe" is well known. "All 'classic,' clean, cut and dried, 'noble,' fixed, 'eternal' *Weltanschauungen* seem to me to violate the character with which life concretely comes and the expression which it bears of being, or at least involving, a muddle and a struggle."[57] This resembles Wright's hatred of the stiff classical and Renaissance traditions in architecture. A dynamic flow—an image of continual becoming—pervades Wright's buildings, and runs equally through James's philosophy. Similarly, Turner's history spoke always of men on the move, venturing westward, breaking the cake of custom, ever engaged in struggle and contradiction. Turner rebelled against the dominant mode of historical scholarship, which emphasized the stability and continuity embodied in the formal structure of institutions. He presented history not as a logical unfolding of constitutions but as a continual flux of experience. In breaking up American history into a balanced interplay of opposing sections,[58] Turner accomplished what James's pluralism achieved in philosophy and what Wright's juxtaposition of advancing and receding planes realized in architecture.

The revolt of these men against intellectual rigidities closely paralleled the assault in popular culture upon a confined and circumscribed life. It is hardly a coincidence that Turner and Theodore Roosevelt made the frontiersman the heroic figure in American history just at the time when he was becoming the hero of best-selling novels. Nor is it happen-stance that Wright did away with interior doors and widened windows just at the time when Edward Bok, editor of the *Ladies' Home Journal,* launched spectacularly successful campaigns to clear out the clutter from parlors and the ugly litter from cities.[59] Like so many other Americans, James, Wright, and Turner were reaching out into the open air.

All three quite literally and passionately loved the out-of-doors. James and Turner were never so happy as when they were camping in the wilderness, and Wright felt as keenly as they the moral strength to be derived from the earth. His prairie houses, stretching outward to embrace the land, attest his fidelity to his mother's injunction, "Keep close to the earth, boy: in that lies strength."[60] For each of these men, nature signified not just power but also the freedom of open space. By explaining American democracy as the product of "free land," Turner extracted a dimension of freedom from the realm of necessity; and this is what Wright did in constructing "the new reality that is *space* instead of matter."[61] Meanwhile, in philosophy, James argued against a restrictive materialism by emphasizing the incompleteness of visible nature and by calling attention to those natural facts of religious experience that suggest a vaster realm of spiritual freedom.[62] In a sense, he too converted matter into space.

In part, the open-air activists of the nineties were harking back to the old American values affirmed by Walt Whitman, the poet who most rapturously identified himself with boundless space.[63] Wright adored Whitman. Turner quoted him. James, the most discriminating of the three, put his finger exactly on Whitman's spaciousness:

> Walt Whitman owes his importance in literature to the systematic expulsion from his writings of all contractile elements. The only sentiments he allowed himself to express were of the expansive order; and he expressed these in the first person, not as your mere monstrously conceited individual might so express them, but vicariously for all men, so that a passionate and mystic ontological emotion suffuses his words. . . .[64]

Appropriately, Whitman's reputation was just then emerging powerfully from the distrustful and evasive gentility that had obscured it earlier. His flowing lines supplied the largeness and virility that more and more Americans wanted in order to overcome the "contractile elements" in late nineteenth century culture. A biography of Whitman published in 1896 by the influential naturewriter John Burroughs made this appeal explicit:

> Did one begin to see evil omen in this perpetual whittling away and sharpening and lightening of the American type,—grace without power, clearness without mass, intellect without character,—then take comfort from the volume and the rankness of Walt Whitman? Did one begin to fear that the decay of maternity and paternity in our older communities and the falling off in the native population presaged the drying up of the race in its very sources? Then welcome to the rank sexuality and to the athletic fatherhood and motherhood celebrated by Whitman. Did our skepticism, our headiness, our worldliness, threaten to eat us up like cancer? Did our hardness, our irreligiousness, and our passion for the genteel point to a fugitive, superficial race? Was our literature threat-

ened with the artistic degeneration—running all to art and not at all to power? Were our communities invaded by a dry rot of culture? Were we fast becoming a delicate, indoor genteel race? Were our women sinking deeper and deeper into the "incredible sloughs of fashion and all kinds of dyspeptic depletion,"—the antidote for all these ills is in Walt Whitman.[65]

Evidently the new appreciation of Whitman, the anti-formalism of James, Wright, and Turner, and the various popular displays of a quasi-primitive vitality arose from a common antipathy toward confinement in life and thought. Evidently also this reaction sprang to a considerable extent from indigenous sources. In fact, the new activism was accompanied by a revulsion against European cultural leadership, and the principal innovators were markedly anti-European in their social and moral attitudes. As a young man Wright refused a splendid opportunity to study architecture in Europe, all expenses paid. He felt, when he did so, that he was "only keeping faith" with America. James, oppressed by the weight of the past world in Europe, returned to the less tradition-laden atmosphere of Harvard, exclaiming, "Better fifty years of Cambridge than a cycle of Cathay."[66] Turner, who conceived of American history as a movement away from Europe, gave our past so native a hue that his successors for half a century treated it as a largely endogenous phenomenon. All of these men associated Europe with the constraint and decrepitude they abhorred. All of them associated America with the freshness and openness they sought to revive.

Nevertheless, their discontents paralleled a similar ferment in European thought and feeling, as we have already noticed in respect to popular culture. In Europe as well as America the balance shifted from a constricting pessimism to a regenerative activism. There, too, the change may be described broadly as a reaction against the stifling atmosphere of bourgeois materialism. Yet the strategy of the rebellion in European high culture had certain distinctive characteristics that may help us to understand the American experience.

A short way of putting the matter is to say that cultural discontent among European intellectuals was more drastic.[67] American intellectuals did not—any more than the American painters of the day—go in for strong colors. One cannot imagine among them a Vincent Van Gogh or a Georges Sorel. Hardly anyone in America directly and belligerently assailed conventional standards of morality. American intellectuals did not, like so many Europeans, feel profoundly alienated from their own society and culture. James, Wright, and Turner conceived of themselves as revitalizing values rooted in American life. Feeling that great reserves of energy lay all around them, they did not look so far afield as those Europeans who turned to primitive myth or to the international proletariat. Nor did they look so far beneath the surface as those Europeans who plunged into the depths of the private self.

Nothing seems more striking in comparative terms than the relative absence in the United States of the radical subjectivity that was entering European thought. In European literature the symbolists were creating an art of equivocality, distortion, and illusion. In philosophy Bergsonian irrationalism and the Nietzschean celebration of the Dionysian ego were beginning to be heard. In psychology Freud was probing the strange world of dreams. In history the leading German theoreticians were declaring their independence from scientific laws and insisting on the subjective basis of historical knowledge. In all these fields, European intellectuals were rending the fabric of external reality and discovering truth in the depths of subjective, personal experience. In America William James, the most precocious and in some ways the most European of our intellectual leaders, was moving in the same direction. For the most part, however, on this side of the Atlantic literature remained realistic, philosophy empirical, psychology behavioral, history scientific. Yet on both continents intellectuals were seeking liberation from closed systems and formalistic abstractions.

The difference may be explained in terms of contrasting environments. America was a big country with a relatively fluid rather than a relatively stable society. In spite of the tightening mesh of institutions, America still offered elbow-room, physically and sociologically. Here the restless intellectual reached outward to the range, flux, and diversity of life around him. In Europe he was more likely to reach inward to the intense and often mystical feelings within himself. Americans rebelled by extending the breadth of experience, Europeans by plumbing its depths. For Americans liberation meant variety, maneuverability, multiplication of the individual's relationships with the world outside himself. Accordingly, James—connoisseur though he was of the "sick soul"—stayed healthy by celebrating multiplicity and constructing an essentially eclectic philosophy. Wright swept away confining walls and opened up fluid space. Turner widened the breadth of history in order to interrelate political, social, economic, and geographical changes.

Unready for the heightened subjectivity of European thought, American intellectuals did not engage in the accompanying criticism of scientific ideas. In Europe objective reality lost some of its authority. Americans, however, resisted sharp segregation between various levels and types of thought: between facts and values, intellect and intuition, the scientific and the supra-scientific. "Something there is that doesn't love a wall," an American poet declared some years later; and the chief American philosophers—James, Dewey, and Peirce—wanted to do away with walls separating subjective values from objective facts. For Americans the external world retained a promise of ultimate goodness and harmony.

Consequently, the broad and various reaches of nature symbolized for the expansive Americans of the 1890's both the vitality they sought and a spacious alternative to the European self-consciousness they shunned. A genteel literary critic of the 1890's, Hamilton Wright Mabie, offers us a final summation of the intellectual strategy that—for better or worse—prevailed:

. . . nothing breeds doubt and despair so quickly as a constant and feverish self-consciousness, with inability to look at life and the world apart from our own interests, emotions, and temperament. This is, in an exceptional degree, an epoch of morbid egoism, of exaggerated and excessive self-consciousness; an egoism which does not always breed vanity, but which confirms the tendency to measure everything by its value to us, and to decide every question on the basis of our personal relation to it. It is always unwise to generalize too broadly and freely about contemporary conditions, but there are many facts to bear out the statement that at no previous period in the history of the world have so many men and women been keenly and painfully self-conscious; never a time when it has been so difficult to look at things broadly and objectively. . . .

From this heated atmosphere and from these representations of disease, put forth as reproductions of normal life, we fly to Nature, and are led away from all thought of ourselves. We escape out of individual into universal life; we bathe in the healing waters of an illimitable ocean of vitality. . . . To drain into ourselves the rivulets of power which flow through Nature, art, and experience, we must hold ourselves open on all sides; we must empty ourselves of ourselves in order to make room for the truth and power which come to us through knowledge and action; we must lose our abnormal self-consciousness in rich and free relations with the universal life around us.[68]

In keeping with his own gentility, Hamilton Wright Mabie softened the outreaching strategy of American culture. For him and for many other Americans it meant escape rather than engagement or rebellion. This was not true, I think, of James or Wright or Turner. But they shared Mabie's confidence in the openness that still redeemed the American situation.

The clear evidence of accommodation and continuity in American culture should not lead us to suppose that the reorientation of the 1890's was unimportant. Even in America the great restlessness that seized the nations of the West toward the end of the nineteenth century has not dissipated itself in dreams of natural harmony or in boasts of physical prowess. The underlying desires and discontents have grown stronger in the twentieth century. If a cultural revolution did indeed begin in the 1890's, its developed proportions and its essential character are only in our own time becoming visible.

# PART III

*Conflict and*

*Consensus*

# 5

---

# THE CONSTRUCTION

# OF AMERICAN HISTORY

*THIS* BRIEF SURVEY *of four centuries of American historiography offers very little that is new or controversial. It provides, however, a general background for the more detailed studies in the following chapters. The text is an updated version of the introductory chapter in* The Reconstruction of American History, *ed. John Higham (London: Hutchinson & Co., 1962), 9–24. Notes have been added.*

T HERE IS A FAIRLY COMMON VIEW, particularly among European intellectuals, that American history is not very interesting and the achievement of American historians not very important. For these disparaging opinions perhaps more can be said than an American scholar likes to admit. Spanning a mere three and a half centuries, American history has no antiquity, few ruins, and little mystery. Moving in a fairly straight line from primitive settlements to triumphant power and plenty, it looks superficially simple. Its complexity lies below the surface and therefore makes a special demand on the historical imagination.

Not having had to wrestle with their history and come to terms with it, Americans themselves have too often taken it for granted. In the eighteenth and nineteenth centuries everwidening opportunities kept most American eyes fixed expectantly upon the future. A pragmatic cast of mind put more emphasis on results than on antecedents. Physical separation from Europe, and repeated declarations of intellectual independence from it, ratified a sense of emancipation from the past. Although history has served almost all Americans as an inspiring chronicle of pride, most of them have undoubtedly turned more readily to other kinds of knowledge to enlarge their range of experience.

One can concede this much but still feel that such easy generalizations tell less than half of the truth. The historical spirit has never lacked sources of strength in American culture, and the alleged "lessons" of history have often made themselves powerfully felt in public affairs. The Constitution itself was framed with the most scrupulous attention to the experience of earlier republics.

Americans have been writing their own history with uninterrupted enthusiasm since it began. In sheer bulk the product equals or surpasses the historical literature on any other modern nation. Since no part of the American past is really remote from the current scene, American history has to an unusual degree a personal and contemporary relevance. Moreover, in almost every generation one or more historians have been among the leading lights of American culture, and their books have exemplified some of its most pronounced characteristics. The writing of American history has always had, therefore, an intimate relation to history in the making.

Historical writing in America falls into three large periods. It began in the seventeenth century as the function of clergymen and of magistrates associated with them in executing the will of God; this was the period of Puritan history. From the early eighteenth to the late nineteenth century, the best history came from the pens of independent gentlemen who did not write in the service of a church or from any other institutional incentive. They had a high respect for the dignity of history, in the writing of which they exhibited a generalized sense of responsibility to society. Theirs was the period of patrician history. Around the end of the nineteenth century, gentlemen-historians yielded predominance to the growing host of university professors, for whom historical activity became a corporate task and specialized career. These men made history once more an institutional product, and such it remains in this century of professional history.

The Puritan fathers of New England deserve the credit for implanting an historical consciousness in the American wilderness. They were neither the first English colonists nor the first to publicize the exploits of Englishmen in the New World. The Elizabethan adventurers who established a foothold in Virginia preceded them, and Captain John Smith's exuberant tract about his first year at Jamestown, *A True Relation* (1608), is probably the earliest English chronicle composed on American soil.[1] But in the southern and middle colonies history seemed useful only as a casual introduction to descriptions of the current scene; until the middle of the eighteenth century, the recording of the past never emerged as a task important in its own right. For New England, however, history supplied an essential vehicle of self-analysis and—after the sermon—one of the principal modes of public discourse.

"It is our great duty," enjoined a Massachusetts clergyman, "to be the Lord's remembrancers or recorders."[2] History told not merely the doings of men; it set forth the actions of God. His will directed every event. The history recorded in scripture and unfolded in subsequent happenings offered the principal clue to His otherwise inscrutable design. To ignore history was to remain in heathen darkness, and to distort or delimit its fullness was self-deceiving. In their passion to tell all, Puritan historians touched on the weather, the state of the crops, crimes, fashions, and business transactions, as well as public events. Their own history in the New World held a special fascination for the Puritans. God had called them to this remote place to complete the Protestant Reformation and thus to lead the way for all mankind. In the grand strategy of history they were enacting the crucial modern chapter. The outcome was uncertain, the record equivocal. They searched it proudly for evidence of their faithfulness and anxiously for signs of their failings.

The most memorable achievements of the Puritan historians

were William Bradford's *Of Plymouth Plantation* and Cotton Mather's *Magnalia Christi Americana*. The first, written piecemeal in the 1630's and 1640's, told the story of the little group of Pilgrims who fled to Holland in 1608 and then settled permanently at Plymouth in 1620. The second, published in 1702, put into a great omnium-gatherum the history of the New England churches and settlements throughout the seventeenth century. Bradford, a plain, self-taught man, was Plymouth's governor for thirty-three years; he took no initiative to publish his writings, and his history remained in manuscript for two centuries. Mather, writing fifty years after Bradford, was Boston's preeminent minister and the most learned American of his day; his printed works included 444 known titles. Bradford set down a straightforward narrative of shared and remembered experience. Mather erected a monument of laborious scholarship to remind a faltering generation of the greatness of its forebears. Bradford combined the simplicity of John Bunyan and the cadence of the English Bible with an effortless grasp of human motivation. Mather united antiquarian fussiness with a pompous delight in classical allusions and metaphysical conceits. But, for all their differences, both books embodied the Puritan's deeply historical sense of destiny and responsibility.

Diffused and secularized, this Puritan legacy persisted after the Church lost its controlling importance in American intellectual life. Throughout the eighteenth and nineteenth centuries the great majority of America's leading historians derived from New England. Some of them—Francis Parkman, George Bancroft, and Richard Hildreth, for example—were sons of New England clergymen. Others, in the New England colleges, got an education steeped in the moral earnestness and cultural traditions of the region. Significantly, New England produced only one major political theorist, John Adams, and he an historical theorist. It produced only one major novelist, Nathaniel Hawthorne, and an historical consciousness profoundly shaped his art. Yet New England produced at least four historians of permanent distinction—Parkman, William H. Prescott, John Lothrop Motley, and Henry Adams. Clearly, the New England intellect distrusted the rational abstractions of political theory and the relaxing temptations and fabrications of the novel. It preferred the solid instruction, the concrete down-to-earth verities, of history. The voice of the Puritan still echoed through the advice that Edwin F. Gay, a prominent twentieth century historian, received as a youth from his father, a lumber magnate of New England descent:

> "Reading is part of the training for life. . . . Now while you are training you should read only what will give you strength; and story books, at least some of them, are cake and pie to you mentally, and take strength from you instead of adding it. You ought not to read them. [Instead,] read histories and travels and lives of great men. Learn to consider what quality of mind or heart made them great or brave or good, and then cultivate those qualities yourself. See where they made mistakes."[3]

The quality of historical writing improved enormously, however, when it no longer had to meet the prescriptions of Puritan theology. In the rationalistic atmosphere of the eighteenth century the desire to fathom the will of God ceased to control the scrutiny of human affairs. Historiography became relatively independent of religious sponsorship, socially as well as intellectually; for a new basis appeared with the accumulation of wealth and leisure in the hands of individuals. Historical scholarship is a laborious, time-consuming enterprise, and a highly cultivated one, not to be expected without access to many books, and opportunity for sustained reflection. Fortunately, in raw, bustling America, a few eighteenth-century gentlemen had good private libraries and some time to spare from an active life to use them.[4] By the middle of the nineteenth century a few men were giving, for long periods, substantially all of their time to history.

The patrician historian had, through pride of ancestry, a sense of personal connection with the past. He responded sympathetically to great occasions and to acts of virtuous individuals. He gave much attention to wars, to the forming of governments, and to the etiquette of public transactions. In appraising the actions of men, he enjoyed a relatively independent stance. Indebted to no one, he felt capable of exercising an unconstrained judgment with entire impartiality. He usually enjoyed playing a judicial role, weighing the evidence, ascribing motives, and pronouncing the magisterial verdict of history. Familiar with the great classical historians, he followed their practice of holding up to posterity examples of errors, failings, and laudable deeds.

Although the patrician historian felt a patriotic pride in free institutions, he generally took the conservative side on most social issues. Typically, he idolized George Washington, disliked Thomas Jefferson, and despised Andrew Jackson. The principal historians writing before and during the American Revolution became loyalists. Later generations inclined first to Federalism, then to Whiggery, and always to the politics of respectability.[5] Accordingly, in the mid-nineteenth century, most historians disapproved of contemporary reform movements, and in the late nineteenth century they firmly opposed the rising economic unrest.

Yet their philosophy of history changed considerably during their long period of dominance. Men of wide culture, the patrician historians kept abreast of European historiography, adopting its advancing methods and changing forms. In the eighteenth century they began to utilize documentary evidence in the careful, critical way already exemplified in Europe by scholarly clerics, such as the Bollandists. They began to make the temperate judgments congenial to an age of reason. They took a new interest in the history of political institutions in the manner of David Hume.

The best of the eighteenth-century historians was Thomas Hutchinson, who wrote a *History of the Colony and Province of Massachusetts-Bay* in three volumes during the decade preceding the American Revolution. In his splendid Boston mansion Hutchinson had gathered an outstanding collection of early manuscript sources. He served as Chief Justice of Massachusetts while writing the first two volumes, and he took special interest in the constitutional and legal history of the province. After an ill-fated interval as royal governor during the deepening revolutionary crisis, he completed his work in unhappy exile. Yet his mind on the whole was unusually irenic and judicious. He appreciated the relativity of customs and standards. He had a shrewd understanding of the arts of political management. He could justly say at one point: "I am not sensible of having omitted any material fact, nor have I designedly given a varnish to the actions of one party, or high coloring to those of the other ... I profess to give a true relation of facts."[6]

In the nineteenth century historians were not content simply to give a true relation of facts, with accompanying conclusions. They became exponents of the concept of development, seeking to exhibit in a coherent, integrated narrative the unfolding continuity of human experience. Now history must reveal not a mere chronological sequence but rather the realization, through connected events, of some underlying principle. Historians therefore organized their books around one or more of the great principles of nineteenth century bourgeois culture: liberty, nationality, and progress.

History cast in a dramatic pattern of development lent itself to the purposes of art; the patrician historian in the nineteenth century regarded himself distinctly as a man of letters. Under the influence of the romantic movement, which greatly heightened appreciation of the past and vitalized its description, good history reached a very large audience. American publishers, pirating cheap editions of Macaulay's history, sold four times as many copies as were distributed in Great Britain, and Prescott's sumptuous *Conquest of Mexico* (1843) enjoyed a comparable success. These writers managed, as no one had before, to re-create with visual immediacy striking scenes and heroic characters.[7]

The romantic approach proved notably congenial to the patrician mind, with its taste for grandeur and its literary inclinations. The only major American historian in the mid-nineteenth century who rejected romanticism was an "outsider," socially unaccepted and intellectually unorthodox. His work was coolly received, and he had to abandon it for lack of support. Richard Hildreth was a pungent anti-slavery and pro-temperance phamphleteer, devoted to Benthamite utilitarianism. His coldly analytical *History of the United States* in six volumes (1849–52), the first scholarly account extending as far as 1821, was remarkable for its realistic interpretations. Hildreth presented American worthies—as he himself said—"unbedaubed with patriotic rouge, wrapped up in no finespun cloaks of excuses and apology, without stilts, buskins, tinsel, or bedizenment, in their own proper persons."[8] He produced the work during an eight-year period when his pretty young wife supported him by painting portraits. Thereafter, to earn a living, he had to return to partisan journalism.

In contrast to Hildreth, another man of modest clerical origins and unorthodox opinions, George Bancroft, gained immense success by adapting himself to the cultural milieu. As a young man ambitious to cut a figure in the world, Bancroft braved the disapproval of Boston society by becoming a professional Democratic politician and writing history with a vague but loud democratic accent. But Bancroft's history glowed with romantic nationalism, and in time its author became a proper gentleman. With the aid of a fortune acquired through marriage and shrewd investments, he withdrew from active politics and from controversy, devoting the rest of a long, distinguished life to his famous *History of the United States from the Discovery of the American Continent* (12 vols., 1834–82).[9]

The last of the romantic historians, Francis Parkman, brought to near-perfection the narrative techniques of that school. His seven-volume *France and England in North America* (1865–92) arrayed French absolutism against Anglo-Saxon liberty in a struggle for control of the American wilderness. Wherever possible, an intrepid individual—La Salle, Frontenac, Montcalm—supplied a focus for the forest drama. No one surpassed Parkman's painstaking research and factual accuracy; no one equalled his feeling for scene and place or his vivid arrangement of action. Unfortunately, a sheltered life and an excessive fixation on martial exploits limited the range of experience in which he could imaginatively participate.[10]

By the 1870's the romantic presuppositions on which Parkman operated were giving way to a positivistic suspicion of such conscious art. Patrician historians still held to the idea of history as narrative, still played the role of men of letters; but they reverted in good measure to Hutchinson's ideal of telling unvarnished facts. Under the spell of scientific thought, historians came to distrust the studied patterns of romantic history, its emphasis on great men, and its pictorial quality. In selecting data, they sought to be more inclusive, in organizing a narrative more open-ended, lest the "real" past be artificially curtailed. In presenting situations, they endeavored to stand apart, observing them from the outside. An array of long, solid histories produced in the eighties and nineties by James Schouler, Justin Winsor, John Bach McMaster, and James Ford Rhodes reflected these changes.[11]

But the new positivistic standards had not yet quite supplanted the older romantic aims. When the tension between the two was acute and sustained, a man might create a masterpiece. Henry Adams had the instincts of an artist together with the philosophy and the analytic intelligence of a scientist. His *History of the United States of America during the Jefferson and Madison Administrations* (9 vols., 1889–91) portrayed a moral drama of individual character against a majestic background of impersonal power. In conception deterministic, in execution full of ambiguity, the work has more than lived up to Adams's boast: "I am writing for a continent of a hundred million people fifty years hence."[12]

From the life of a literary gentleman in Washington, Adams departed for a few years in the 1870's, when he taught the first historical seminar in an American university. Thus he bridged the social transition from patrician to professional history, just as he straddled the intellectual divide between romanticism and science. The modern American university grew up during Adams's lifetime, and Americans who studied in Germany transplanted to it the canons of professional history. Restrictions that Adams could tolerate only briefly became the terms on which historical scholarship underwent a great transformation.

The immediate consequence of professionalization was a more radical and decisive thrust in the direction in which the patrician historians were moving. While patrician history retained a discursive, narrative form, the professionals disclaimed all literary pretensions. They conceived of themselves as scientists. "The old union between history and literature is now broken in all the growing colleges," Carl Becker was told in 1896, when he was selecting his graduate studies at the University of Wisconsin.[13] To achieve a thoroughly positivistic history, the professionals put great emphasis on critical examination of original texts, on checking evidence, and on bibliographical apparatus. To penetrate as deeply as possible into past events, they welcomed specialization and wrote monographs on carefully limited subjects. To cleanse scholarship of the subjective coloration of the historian's own personality, the professionals endeavored to banish the function—so dear to patrician hearts—of passing moral judgments on men and movements.

This whole program heightened uniformity in historical writing at the cost of individuality. The other side of specialization was co-operation. Professional historians sought to integrate their activities through such devices as the seminar, the learned society, the scholarly journal, and the Dewey decimal system for libraries. To synthesize monographic research and to handle subjects beyond the reach of any single specialist, they began to publish collaborative works. Thus, the coming of age of professional history was signalled by the publication of the *American Nation* series (1904–07), in which twenty-four authors contributed separate volumes to a single history of the United States.

In addition to its scientific emphasis, professional history had another consequence, not so quickly apparent but in the long run equally important. In time, the new conditions facilitated a great democratization of historical scholarship. Institutionalized in a vast educational system, research became a possible and attractive career for men of many sorts and conditions. It ceased to be a near monopoly of a patrician class. Students who came to history from diverse backgrounds brought with them a sympathetic interest in aspects of the past beyond the patrician's range of vision.

The full impact of this wider interest was not felt until after 1910, because the first generation of professional historians pursued the narrowly institutional studies they had learned to cultivate in Germany. The second generation, trained in American graduate schools, turned attention toward popular movements, social processes, and economic conflicts. Even George Bancroft, in tone the most democratic of the nineteenth century historians, had merely celebrated democracy as an abstract principle while actually writing about a ruling elite. From 1910 to 1945, however, many professional historians took as their theme the functioning of a democratic society. They did so with an egalitarian commitment to protest and reform, and to that extent compromised the ethical neutrality desired by the scientific school.

This change occurred under the favoring influence of the Progressive movement, which shaped the mind and politics of the early twentieth century, survived the 1920's, and enjoyed a renaissance in an altered form during Franklin D. Roosevelt's New Deal. The democratic emphasis in historiography during those years flourished under the leadership of two great historians: first, Frederick Jackson Turner; later, Charles A. Beard. Both were middle-class Middle Westerners. Although Turner concentrated on the sectional opposition of West to East and Beard on the conflict of classes, both found the main theme of American history in the struggle between under- and over-privileged groups. Neither had much sympathy for the moneyed and patrician groups of the East.

After World War II a third generation of professional historians came to the fore. Its intellectual strategies are discussed in other chapters. Here I shall simply list a few ways in which the third generation has moved from the posture of the second.

1. *No great leaders.* In contrast to the second generation, the third has not produced a decisive leadership. We have no Turner, no Beard to rally around. The postwar generation overhauled the interpretive structure that Turner and Beard built; new hypotheses replaced parts of their work. But another framework for American history as impressive and substantial as theirs once seemed has not materialized. Suppleness, critical awareness, and a search for new formulations characterize recent scholarship. Agreement is to be found largely in the recognition of common problems and the sharing of common moods, not in a unifying principle of explanation.

2. *Attraction of intellectual history.* A special interest in American intellectual history actually dates from the heyday of the second generation, during the 1920's and 1930's. For the vast majority of historians then, however, ideas had a distinctly subordinate status in historical reality. Tangible, external things, like economic interest

and environmental conditions, seemed more important. The third generation of professional historians has largely given up its predecessor's belief in the preponderance of material forces in history. We have no alternative theory of causation; but much of our energy has gone into discovering the subjective meaning that events had for participants.

3. *Rejection of economic interpretations.* The swing toward intellectual history is one of the factors that have diverted scholars from economic interpretations of American history. Another reason is the hugely satisfying performance of the American economy in the 1940's and after. Historians interpret the past most readily in the light of the concerns uppermost in their present. After the war, questions about national values, about the individual's place in a mass society, or about international relations seemed more urgent than difficulties in the production and distribution of income. Accordingly, the emphasis that many historians a generation ago put on economic motives for the Puritan migration to New England, the outbreak of the American Revolution, the writing of the Constitution, the Civil War, imperialism, and American entrance into World War I, has been superseded. In fact, historians now distrust all impersonal, deterministic explanations. They try to take account of economic influences, not as sovereign forces with a preordained outcome, but as part of the complex and unstable make-up of particular human beings.

4. *The contradictions of American experience.* If no single interpretation of American history stands out today, have we arrived at least at a comprehensive image of our past? The most influential historians of the second generation described an America divided between the democratic many and the privileged few. Has the third generation fixed upon another design? For a time it seemed so. In breaking away from the great progressive historians, the third generation produced in the 1950's a conservative design that minimized the magnitude of social conflict in American history and depicted favorably a relatively homogeneous society. Nevertheless, the theme of conflict was far from exhausted. Some historians have attempted to combine such antithetical principles as consensus and conflict

without entirely negating either alternative. Like modern literary critics and theologians, they seem to say that life is ambiguous. America becomes a realm of paradox: a nation born of a revolt that was moderate, yet genuinely revolutionary; a society liberal in its ideals yet conservative in its behavior; a land knit together and fragmented in perplexing ways. More recently young radical scholars have found themselves unable to agree on the nature or extent of the American consensus. Never has the American past seemed more complex, contradictory, and unsettled than it does today.

5. *Decline and revival of "scientific" history.* The narrowly scientific outlook that the first generation of professional historians adopted has undergone a slow but relentless revision. Some of the leaders of the second generation, notably Beard and Carl Becker, questioned the feasibility and the conservative implications of the ideal of rigid objectivity. In their later years they tried to reestablish the old nineteenth century connection of history with philosophy and literature. Many in the third generation have gone further in this direction without necessarily sharing Beard's spirit of protest and reform. Instead of trying to stand entirely outside of the subject under investigation, today's historians commonly attempt to see events through the eyes of participants. They are also more willing than formerly to venture unprovable speculations. On the other hand, a growing minority of scholars in recent years has regretted that the historical profession strayed from its early scientific aspirations. They have proclaimed, and to some extent practiced, a new scientific history, which is not content with the organized accumulation of factual knowledge. Instead, they seek quite deliberately to test the historical limits of hypotheses about human behavior and thus to function as social scientists working in the dimension of time. Many in this group put a high premium on quantitative measurement in order to make precise statements about large masses of people and long-term trends. Thus, a contrast between humanistic and scientific approaches to history has become once again a major issue, though most historians locate themselves somewhere between the two extremes.

# 6

## THE DIVIDED LEGACY OF FREDERICK JACKSON TURNER

No AMERICAN HISTORIAN *has been more written about than Frederick Jackson Turner. My intention is simply to bring the discussion of his ideas up to date. Since this piece was written during a residence of several months in England, I found a trans-Atlantic perspective on the American frontier engaging. Printed originally under the title "The Old Frontier" in the* New York Review of Books, *April 25, 1968, pp. 10–14, this review essay has been expanded somewhat, and footnotes have been added.*

How IMPORTANT was the western movement in shaping American history and forming a distinctive national character? For three decades, from the 1930's through the 1950's, specialists in American history argued the issue fiercely. On the whole, southern and western scholars held faithfully to the teachings of the master, Frederick Jackson Turner. In opposition to this "Turnerverein," to recall some of the epithets of the day, arose the "asphalt flowers," men who identified with a cosmopolitan, urban culture, and who regarded Turner's view of American history as a kind of rural provincialism writ large. Surely American democracy had not come "stark and strong and full of life, from the American forest," as Turner declared in one of his more enthusiastic moments.[1] It was the creation of prophets far more than pioneers, of statesmen rather than backwoodsmen. It was above all the unfolding of an inheritance rather than the flowering of an environment. It came not from nature but from civilization.

This was a ranging, searching debate. The Turner Thesis concerning the influence of the frontier offered the only comprehensive, distinctive interpretation of the whole of American history, so the controversy about it touched every scholar and reacted upon every view of the historical process. Yet the argument never spread beyond the confines of American universities. In the popular mind the vision of the pioneer as the quintessential American remained firmly entrenched. Moreover, the world outside the United States kept much the same image. American scholars might attack the frontier theory as parochial, even isolationist; they might insist that it perpetuated an indigenous, primitive Americanism and thus neglected the interconnections between the United States and Europe; but trans-Atlantic students of American institutions paid little heed. They continued—those who were not Marxists—serenely to follow Frederick Jackson Turner.[2] If the Europe-centered critics had really won the argument at home, they would then have had the task of converting the Europeans as well.

Actually, we owe to a European-born and educated journalist the most impressive anticipation of Turner's theory. In an essay published in 1865, E.L. Godkin, the brilliant founding editor of *The Nation,* set forth the first systematic appraisal of the impact of the frontier on American habits of thought. Godkin's sympathies, to be sure, were decidedly different from Turner's. A patrician liberal of the school of John Stuart Mill, Godkin associated himself with every effort to civilize the rough and turbulent America of his day—to curb its anarchic individualism, its all-absorbing passion for material gain, its often crude anti-intellectualism—and thus to reconstitute the authority of a cultivated elite in a democratic society. Troubled by the unattractive features of American democracy, the young

Anglo-Irish immigrant was nonetheless convinced that those features were transitory. His 1865 essay, "Aristocratic Opinions of Democracy," sought to refute Alexis de Tocqueville's charge that democracy is inseparable from mediocrity, materialism, and disrespect for authority. Not so, Godkin asserted. These qualities derive from frontier conditions. The West

has succeeded to a certain extent in propagating in the East its ideas and manners, both political and social. . . . It now supplies our Presidents, a large body of our legislators, and a large portion of our army. It gives its tone to the national thought, and its direction to the national policy. As might be expected, it has, with its rude, wild energy, its excess of animal life, completely overwhelmed the thinkers of the older States, and driven most of them into private life, and taken upon itself to represent American democracy to the world. American democracy is thus made answerable by superficial observers for faults which flow not from its own nature, but from the outward circumstances of some of those who live under it.[3]

America could be redeemed, since its vices were not rooted in the essential principles of democracy. Those vices belonged instead to an early and passing phase of social evolution.

During the ensuing years, when industrialization seemed to intensify all the qualities that Godkin despised, his youthful optimism about democracy and about post-frontier America drained away. He turned to gloomier explanations of the problems of the day; and it remained for the celebrants rather than the opponents of the frontier to elaborate further on its importance. Thus Turner, writing with a deep love of the West and of its people, advanced in 1893 an account of what the frontier did to America that was in some ways very similar to Godkin's. But Turner described as desirable and lasting the traits the frontier bred. For the young Wisconsin historian the democratic tide in America owed to the frontier not just its turbid violence but its very being.

Neither Godkin nor Turner could satisfactorily explain the persistence of supposedly frontier traits in the new America of the late nineteenth and twentieth centuries. Indeed, Turner had assigned to an immediate environmental setting so decisive a role as to make the survival of the frontier heritage in another setting logically implausible. His critics have made much of this difficulty, pointing out that the thesis rested on a geographical determinism. To the extent that American democracy sprang from the frontier, it should decline with the passing of the frontier.[4] But Turner, unlike Godkin, never lost faith in democracy or in America. The Turner Thesis was more than a scientific hypothesis. It was also a declaration of faith, a romantic invocation of a great national experience, phrased in allusive terms that have provoked endless exegesis and disagreement. Moreover, it was a challenging invitation to historians to look away from laws and constitutions and find in the actions of ordinary people the meaning of American history.

In popular addresses Turner frequently reiterated his vision of the wilderness transforming the European settler into an American; but his research efforts soon turned toward a more tangible, concrete problem. Striving for greater precision, he shifted from an emphasis on the frontier as such to an analysis of sections, particularly in their interplay with one another.[5] Unfortunately this aspect of Turner's thought—so promising in its implications for a comparative history of regional and local cultures in the United States—never came to fruition. It remained inconclusive in Turner's own work, vitiated perhaps by his geophysical presuppositions; and among his successors the sectional approach gradually lost a broadly comparative reference. It became focused on the examination of a few major sectional conflicts; or it narrowed to a specialized scrutiny of the history of a single area, notably of course the West.

Thus Turner left a divided heritage. On the one hand he provided a general theory, of interest to everyone, about the influence of the frontier process on the whole of American life. On the other hand, he raised up a small army of scholars preoccupied with cowboys, Indians, agrarian unrest, and other supposedly distinctive features of the history of the West. It is a pity that these two interests, so insecurely joined in Turner's own mind, persisted among his successors side by side without a genuinely critical interaction. Instead of inspiring an analysis of different types of communities and their characteristic patterns of growth, the frontier theory simply gave academic respectability to the classic story of exploit and struggle among the men who ventured westward. By the 1930's hardly a university beyond the Appalachians lacked an advanced course on the History of the American West. Such courses depended more or less slavishly on Turner's original formulation of 1893 for their unifying principles and their claim to historical significance.

Accordingly, when this interpretation of American history came under sharp attack about a generation ago, the assault did not arise primarily from the study of the West. In general, it took the form of a sweeping impatience with the whole frontier school and a desire to give priority to subjects that could not be justly appreciated from an orthodox western point of view. Intellectual history, international politics, the growth of cities, the challenge of industrialism, the trauma of race, the anguish of disillusion: these were the great themes that now clamored for attention.

The criticism of what historians had neglected under the spell of Turner was incontrovertible; the dissatisfaction was liberating. But the onslaught, for all its vigor and variety, improved very little on Turnerian scholarship in defining relations between East and West or between old and new communities. In fact the attack on Turner really discouraged a systematic rethinking of his ideas, except as they bore on the increasingly fascinating question of national character. Scholarly interest turned away from the sectional conflicts and regional diversities Turner had posited. In a dreary era of consensus, America was coming to seem a much more homogeneous country, more uniform and more stable, than Turner had imagined, and that was undoubtedly one important reason for the decline of his influence.

Although the rest of the world, as I have said, still cherished the frontier legend, during the 1940's and 1950's the critics forced a general recognition among professional historians in the United States that Turner had vastly overstated his case. Insofar as "the existence of an area of free land" did (in Turner's words) "explain American development," the land must have become free—or rather widely available—because of policies and values brought to it. A little comparison with frontiers in other countries made clear the importance of the cultural heritage. Moreover, frontier society proved to be much less "free" than Turner had supposed. It was in many ways highly imitative of eastern culture; and everywhere it quickly manifested some of the common social inequalities of American life, including farm tenancy, urban elites, and corporate power.

Nevertheless, the frontier hypothesis would not die, for what was there to replace it? The critics, though effective in negative ways and in stimulating other lines of inquiry, had less success in giving an alternative explanation of what was unique about American history and the American character. Increasingly, a fascination with the distinctive role of the United States in the modern world drove scholars back to Turner's implicit concern with national differences. Or, more precisely, one might say that it was now Godkin's question that was posed anew: what accounts for the *special features* of American democracy—its peculiar blend of individualism and conformity, its taste for violence, its propensity for informal cooperation, its distrust of theory? This question in turn has led to international comparisons of an increasingly sophisticated kind. As a consequence one of the remarkable trends in American historiography during the 1950's was the emergence of some elegant, highly modernized reformulations of the frontier hypothesis. The results to date may be studied in part in Ray Billington's *America's Frontier Heritage* (1966) and in an anthology of scholarly essays edited by Richard Hofstadter and Seymour Lipset.

Billington is perhaps the most widely respected of our frontier historians; for he writes vigorously upon large themes while maintaining a scrupulous fidelity to detail. Located at the Huntington Library, he occupies the post that Turner held after retiring from Harvard. His latest book, based on recent scholarship and on his own very extensive research, makes a full-dress reappraisal of Turner's claims for the influence of the frontier. Always temperate and judicious, Billington's fundamental strategy concedes the partial truth of all the criticisms but contends that they leave undamaged a vital margin of validity at almost every point in Turner's argument. Thus Billington recognizes that Turner saw the frontier in too rosy a light; so he gives more attention (though not enough in my opinion) to such unattractive "frontier" traits as lawlessness, wastefulness, and anti-intellectualism. Billington admits that Turner employed a vague, metaphorical terminology, but indicates how his propositions can be recast in language more acceptable to contemporary social scientists. For example, Turner sometimes seemed to assign a magical potency to nature—to the physical environment— but the frontier can be rightly understood as a social environment offering a maximum opportunity for initiative and self-advancement. Billington appreciates, moreover, that many ingredients other than the frontier have entered into the making of American civilization; so he eschews any exclusive claims. He acknowledges that the new tendencies fostered by the westward movement were often subtle matters of degree rather than kind, and so insists only that "there is a slight distinction between" American and European democracy.

It is hard to quarrel with such a sound, cautious book—hard indeed to feel excited at all. *America's Frontier Heritage* brings the case for the frontier up to date; yet it remains essentially a defense of an established position. By undertaking a running commentary on a complex debate over a congeries of loosely connected propositions, Billington has not allowed himself to explore any single point in depth. We encounter the intellectual energy and excitement of the controversy more directly in the Hofstadter and Lipset reader, *Turner and the Sociology of the Frontier* (1968).

This is not in itself a particularly noteworthy book. The historiographical introduction by Hofstadter provides only a casual summary. The brief sociological appraisal by Lipset simply repeats some material already published in a longer article under another title in a different book.[6] There is no bibliography, nor do the editors venture any estimate of the present state of the question. Indeed, the true role of the frontier, its real importance in American experience, is not what primarily interests them. They have brought together some recent interpretations of the frontier to illustrate a fruitful convergence between history and sociology. (The book under review comprises the second half of a two-volume set, *The Sociology of*

*American History,* of which the first volume is more broadly concerned with methodology.) The editors have simply collected an array of stimulating articles, first published in scholarly journals between 1941 and 1961, which illuminate the decline and revival of the frontier idea. We are left to draw our own conclusions.

On one point no doubt is permitted: the revival owed much to the contributions of social scientists. The conceptual resources of economists and sociologists have helped us to see the frontier as the expanding perimeter of a growth process affecting the whole society. Thus, for instance, two economists, George G. S. Murphy and Arnold Zellner, apply modern growth theory to Turner's supposedly discredited idea of the frontier as a safety-valve for industrial discontent. Their essay brilliantly demonstrates how nineteenth century America attained an exceptionally high rate of investment and per capita income through repeated additions of geographical areas capable of supporting industrialization.

But in estimating the significance of the frontier, this kind of analysis involves us in a puzzling ambiguity. On the one hand, the westward movement seems to be restored to central importance in American history. This is because the advance of settlement into the empty West stands out as the cardinal dimension of a pervasive mobility—a venturesome, risk-taking, migratory style of life—which had become by the nineteenth century the dominant feature of American society. Everything that we regard for better or worse as uniquely American has been shaped by our characteristic mobility and so appears in boldest relief in the frontier process.

On the other hand, such an approach deprives the westward movement of the autonomous role Turner assigned to it. Absorbed into a larger theory of "mobility," it is reduced to a special case of a more general phenomenon; and the search for explanation turns in directions that may lead far from the frontier. Controversy subsides, for all the distinctions—between inheritance and environment, between East and West, between rural and urban migration, between Turnerians and anti-Turnerians—tend to dissolve as we stand transfixed before the enveloping spectacle of American mobility. That, at least, is the current state of the matter. And there it is likely to remain so long as the uniformities of American character and experience obscure the other half of Turner's heritage, his interest in group contrasts and regional diversities.[7] Until historians attend more closely to such differences we shall not distinguish satisfactorily between the westward movement and the other energies of a dynamic society.

Indeed, it may be too much to expect that either half of Turner's divided legacy can flourish in the immediate future. Neither the nationalism of the frontier thesis nor the regionalism of the sectional approach appeals very strongly to the American mind in the late 1960's. None of the articles reprinted by Hofstadter and Lipset was written more recently than 1960. The sociological re-examination of frontier theory seems to have petered out about the time when social psychologists and historians drifted away from the study of national character. Possibly historians are tiring of the frontier thesis because we have stopped congratulating ourselves on the national traits the frontier allegedly fostered; and the sectional approach fails to revive because the social differences that agitate Americans now do not arise primarily from their regional locations.

A look at the present cultural context also helps to explain the lull in Turnerian scholarship. Not only among scholars but also in American popular culture the myth of the frontier may be losing much of its old magic. In spite of some fanfare by the publisher, Billington's new book got almost no attention from general reviewers. At a broader level, one must look hard these days to find a western story on the paperback book rack or among the new movies. On the screen the western's decline in popularity goes back to the latter half of the 1950's, when western films dropped from one quarter of Hollywood's total output to less than one tenth. Television, as usual, has lagged behind, but here, too, the western vogue faded rapidly in the late 1960's.

Efforts at revitalizing the genre have succeeded chiefly in unsettling its traditional moral vision. In the classic western story men enacted a ritual of social purification and renewal in a realm of boundless space. Metro-Goldwyn-Mayer tried in 1963 to do something of the sort again in a multimillion-dollar epic, *How the West*

*Was Won,* designed to resuscitate the western film. Through an evident incapacity on the part of the producers to believe in what they were saying, the picture went awry and ended in jarring scenes of superhighways and bulldozers.[8] A few years later, in *Easy Rider* (1969), the western myth became a poignant, mocking memory, now finally blasted for roving adventurers and conformist townsmen alike. As I pointed out in Chapter 4, Turner's announcement of the significance of the frontier was part of a general rediscovery of the youthfulness and openness of American experience. It is necessary to ask if today's Americans are losing Turner's underlying faith in the relevance of the pioneer heritage. Are the American people giving up their most cherished myth?

Among serious scholars, of course, the writing of western history goes on, though increasingly in a non-Turnerian context. It is an industry stimulated in many colleges and universities, from the Appalachians to the Sierras, by local pride and the availability of source material. Styles of scholarship in this genre change slowly. But here too historians in recent years have shown increasing interest in those aspects of western history that are national—not uniquely western—in scope. While generalists were redefining the frontier as a special instance of American mobility, western specialists have focused on topics like the rise of cities and the penetration of outside culture and capital into the western scene. The most impressive new book of that sort is William H. Goetzmann's *Exploration and Empire,* an imposing narrative of the expeditions and travels during the nineteenth century that opened up the land beyond the great bend of the Missouri River.[9]

On the subject of exploration the literature already available is enormous. Scholars as well as antiquarians have patiently tracked the footsteps of hundreds of explorers. Goetzmann, however, supplies the first account that is both panoramic and detailed. His book with its abundant pictures and maps (the latter so reduced as to be frequently illegible) will stand for a long time as a major work of synthesis and reference. What makes it also a fresh approach to the subject is the author's attempt to understand exploration against the background of the unfolding objectives and capacities of the national culture. Here the explorer is not an independent adventurer, enclosed in his western habitat. He is the agent of a pre-existing civilization, guided by its knowledge and curiosity and backed by its organizational strength. Through these pages pass a succession of army officers serving the purposes of American imperialism, fur trappers who carry with them a range of entrepreneurial ambitions, soldier-engineers trained at West Point, artists inspired by romantic exoticism, and scientists probing for geological and ethnological discoveries. The story begins with the Lewis and Clark Expedition of 1804; it ends with the retirement in 1894 of John Wesley Powell as Director of the U.S. Geological Survey. Throughout, the importance of governmental sponsorship is emphasized.

Few will want such abundant detail. For less industrious readers the same enthusiastic publisher of frontier Americana, Alfred A. Knopf, has obligingly brought out another volume, equally lavish but not so demanding. *America's Western Frontiers* by John A. Hawgood deals with the settlement as well as the exploration of the Trans-Mississippi West.[10] We meet, along with some of the better known explorers and trappers, the whole cast of characters who populate the standard, well-loved story of the West: the wagoneers thronging the emigrant trails, the rousting argonauts of the Gold Rush, the great railroad builders, the valiant Indian chiefs of the Plains, the doughty Mormons, the cattlemen, and finally (a slight letdown) the plain American homesteaders.

Hawgood has no lust for new interpretations; he writes entirely from a conventional point of view. Yet his scholarship is sound and his narrative studded with diverting anecdotes. The book may be read for information and pleasure. It may also be seen as further evidence that the epic of the American frontier, in spite of all conceptual difficulties, remains a highly exportable cultural resource. After roaming for many years across the land he describes so affectionately, Professor Hawgood proudly inscribed his preface at the Placer Hotel, Last Chance Gulch, Helena, Montana; but he is in fact an English historian, educated at London and Heidelberg, who teaches at the University of Birmingham in the heart of industrial

Britain. In an increasingly denationalized world, it would be a salutary irony if trans-Atlantic scholars should do us the service of keeping alive our most distinctive myth, and if eventually another Godkin should discover a new, unsuspected relevance in Turner's legacy.

# 7

## CHARLES A. BEARD:
## A SKETCH

THERE IS NOW FROM *Richard Hofstadter a searching critique of Beard's major books, and I have written in* History *(1965) at some length about his influence. The only brief synthesis of Beard's whole career, however, is this biographical article, which I reprint from* International Encyclopedia of the Social Sciences *([New York, 1968], II, 33–37; copyright 1968 by Crowell Collier and Macmillan, Inc.).*

*My greatest assistance in gathering the facts and assimilating the flavor of Beard's life came from his daughter, Miriam Vagts, and her husband, Alfred, who gave me a delightful lunch and an entire afternoon at their home near New Milford, Connecticut, where Beard's farm was located. I am grateful to them. I am grateful also for my own memories of Beard as a teacher and an awesome personality, when he occupied a professorial chair at Johns Hopkins in 1940–41. Beard arrived with grandiose intentions of creating a great school of American historical studies. It was a bruising year. He was engaged in a bitter foreign policy fight; the vast majority of the faculty were on the other side. The following summer a student visiting New Milford asked if Beard would ever return to Hopkins.*

*"If [President] Isaiah Bowman pushed a peanut with his nose all the way from Baltimore to New Milford to ask me," the old man snorted,*

*"I would refuse." He raised his eyes to the horizon. "These are my hills.
They shall not take me from my hills again."*
*They never did.*

N OT ONLY AS AN HISTORIAN but also as a political scientist and edu-
cator, Charles A. Beard was one of the most influential social thinkers in the United States from about 1912 to 1941. He helped to
transform the discipline of political science in the early twentieth
century. Later, between the two world wars, he came close to dom-
inating the study of American history. He was ranked by a group of
liberal intellectuals of that era as second only to Thorstein Veblen
among the writers who had influenced their thought, and in a poll
taken by *Survey* magazine, shortly after Beard's death, a group of
editors and educators voted his masterpiece, *The Rise of American
Civilization* (1927), the book that best explained American democracy. Altogether, he published over three hundred articles and about
sixty books, some in collaboration with his wife, Mary Ritter Beard,
some with other associates. His textbooks on European and American history and on American government sold many millions of
copies. The product of an age of reform, he was always the scholar
*engagé,* assailing conventional myths and shibboleths, pronouncing
continually on current events, and plunging repeatedly into policy
making. The force of his personality penetrated not only his writings
but every dimension of his life; for Beard enjoyed his power and
bore himself with the authority of an ancient sage.

The son of a substantial landowner and building contractor,
Beard was born in 1874, and then brought up, on a farm near
Knightstown, Indiana. His parents were old-fashioned rationalists
and descendants of Quakers; this heritage gave Beard a lifelong
sense of close personal and intellectual kinship with eighteenth
century America. The down-to-earth, humane cast of mind that he
derived from his upbringing was broadened at DePauw University
through acquaintance with the writings of Karl Marx and especially
John Ruskin, whose portrait always hung in Beard's study. A sum-

mer in Chicago, spent partly at Hull House, brought Beard into direct involvement with current social unrest. On graduating from DePauw in 1898, he went to England to study English and European history at Oxford. There he associated with cosmopolitan and radical spirits and had a large share in organizing a workingmen's college, Ruskin Hall. His first book, *The Industrial Revolution* (1901), explained current social problems to British working-class readers. His Oxford experience gave Beard a considerable familiarity with English literary culture, a distinctly uncommon attribute among American social scientists.

These moral and humane enthusiasms came increasingly under the discipline of an austere scientific methodology. From his Oxford professors, notably Frederick York Powell, Beard learned of the growing aspiration for a science of man that would furnish empirical understanding of human affairs without the intrusion of value judgments. Further graduate study at Columbia University, where Beard acquired the Ph.D. degree in 1904, confirmed his adherence to a value-free social science.

From one point of view Beard's whole career can be seen as a struggle to maintain a fruitful union between his belief in science as a rigidly objective inquiry and his ardent commitment to moral action.

At Columbia in the early twentieth century, such a union was not hard to maintain. Empiricism was then the watchword throughout the social sciences in America, and at Columbia Beard joined a notable company of scholars who were convinced that the advance of democracy depended on a social science that would replace dogmatic or speculative statements with concrete, practical knowledge of particular situations and techniques. This view—at once scientific, utilitarian, and "present-minded"—was spelled out in philosophy by John Dewey and in history by James Harvey Robinson. The latter propounded a "New History," which would be a synthesis of the results of more specialized sciences and which would thereby reach out into the whole context of human activity instead of dwelling on the slow unfolding of formal institutions. New Historians would study the technique of progress and, in general, concentrate on the aspects of the past most relevant to the great public problems of the present. Thus Robinson's history emphasized change rather than continuity and invoked the authority of science for the reform of scholarship and society. All of this appealed strongly to Beard, who grew rapidly from a protégé to a partner of the older man.

Although Beard's training was primarily in history, his appointment at Columbia after 1907 was in the department of public law. Over the next decade his teaching and writing related primarily to American constitutional history and public administration. He constantly stressed the social and economic "realities" discoverable behind legal principles and governmental forms. To Beard the abandonment of an abstract, largely a priori analysis of law and sovereignty permitted political science to look more closely into motives, interests, and practical results. In the new field of public administration his work was very practical indeed. As a leader in the pioneering New York Bureau of Municipal Research, he directed a number of major state and municipal surveys designed to rationalize governmental machinery and establish clear criteria of public responsibility. Later, in 1922–23, he acted as adviser to the Bureau of Municipal Research in Tokyo and also advised the Japanese government on the rebuilding of the city after a disastrous earthquake.

In constitutional history Beard's research flowed from an equally practical, contemporary interest. A series of conservative, laissez-faire decisions by the Supreme Court had aroused a heated debate over its legitimate powers. In *The Supreme Court and the Constitution* (1912) Beard made a more intensive investigation than anyone had previously done of the intentions of the Founding Fathers with respect to judicial review. He concluded that the framers had intended the Supreme Court to exercise control over legislation. Judicial control was just one facet of the larger purpose of the framers to protect property rights against turbulent popular majorities. Yet Beard ended by acclaiming the tough-minded intelligence with which the makers of the Constitution grounded it on the rock of self-interest. Where others discerned idealism, Beard saw a more praiseworthy realism.

Beard's most famous monograph, *An Economic Interpretation of the Constitution* (1913), examined with care the Founding Fathers' motives. Inspired partly by the quantitative studies of sectional voting patterns that Frederick Jackson Turner and his students were making, Beard surveyed the distribution of economic power in the United States in 1787 and itemized the property holdings of every delegate to the Constitutional Convention of that year. He concluded that at least five-sixths of the delegates stood to gain personally from the adoption of the Constitution, chiefly because it would protect the public credit and raise the value of the public securities they held. This thesis was a striking demonstration of a research technique— collective biography—that has only recently come into common use in historical studies; but Beard's analytical design seems crude compared to subsequent refinements. He proceeded as if conscious material self-interest were the only determinant of political behavior and thus assumed what he proposed to demonstrate. Moreover, he imposed a simplistic social dualism on his findings about individuals: he presented the Constitution as the instrument of capitalistic creditors arrayed against landowning debtors. Beard further documented the same cleavage in a third significant monograph, *Economic Origins of Jeffersonian Democracy* (1915). Here he tried to demonstrate that the alignment of 1787 reappeared in the political parties of the 1790's: Jeffersonian democracy simply meant the transfer of federal power from the holders of fluid capital to the agriculturalists.

In the writing of American history Beard's capitalist-agrarian dichotomy quickly assumed immense importance, for it asserted a pattern of conflict that was refreshingly "realistic" without being alien to traditional American political rhetoric. In effect, Beard's economic interpretation of American history provided a tangible class basis for the old idea that American politics was essentially a contest between Jeffersonian democracy and Hamiltonian privilege. By postulating a basic antagonism between two coalitions of interest groups, one dominated by urban capitalists, the other by farmers and planters, he used a flexible dualism in place of the more complex Marxist scheme that was influencing the writing of European history.

During the 1920's and 1930's the best of the books Beard wrote, together with those of such major scholars as Vernon L. Parrington, Arthur M. Schlesinger, and Howard K. Beale, amplified this conceptual scheme. Thus Beard's *The Idea of National Interest* (1934) contrasted Hamiltonian with Jeffersonian traditions of foreign policy and grounded each in economic interests. The capitalist-agrarian struggle also supplied the underlying dynamics for *The Rise of American Civilization* (1927). Among the special features of this panoramic volume were an interpretation of Jacksonian democracy as a farmer-labor uprising and a view of the Civil War as a "Second American Revolution," in which northern businessmen drove the planter aristocracy from power.

Yet there were significant differences between *The Rise of American Civilization* and Beard's prewar writings. He had resigned from Columbia in 1917 in protest against wartime infringements on academic freedom, and during the 1920's he became deeply disturbed both by the threat that modern war posed to democratic values and by the loss of confidence in progress and human nature then spreading in many intellectual circles. Instead of simply trusting in scientific inquiry to solve social problems, Beard began explicitly to defend his basic values. Living independently in the hills of Connecticut, he was increasingly removed from the behavioralist trend in political science; his writing assumed a more humanistic cast. *The Rise of American Civilization* combined the economic determinism he had developed before the war with an unashamed celebration of the cultural achievements of the American people. Specifically, it vindicated their collective energy and their undaunted faith in progress.

The depression and the spread of totalitarianism intensified Beard's concern with values. His herculean activities in the 1930's were an attempt to reanimate in America by creative thought the progress that science and world history no longer seemed to assure. In *The Open Door at Home* (1934) and other writings he sketched an ambitious blueprint for a planned economy. He exercised a major and perhaps decisive influence on the sixteen-volume *Report* of the American Historical Association's Commission on the Social Studies in the Schools, 1932–37, which declared that education in primary and secondary schools should be attuned to the advance of collectivistic democracy. He became the principal intellectual spokesman of isolationism. And he began to study the philosophy of history.

Until the 1930's very few American scholars in any discipline had paid serious attention to the basic problems of historical thought. Pragmatic Americans accepted science rather than philosophy as the key to historical knowledge. While Beard continued to insist that history must be useful, he now declared that it could not also be scientific and objective and that it must cease to be deterministic. His thunderous address as president of the American Historical Association, "Written History as an Act of Faith" (1934), urged historians to recognize the subjectivity of history in order to restore the primacy of values in the study of man and thereby guide history in the making.

Beard's loss of confidence in the ability of scientific techniques to solve the great problems of the day inspired a general revolt against scientific history. His new conception of history, along with similar views expressed by Carl Becker, plunged U.S. historians into a great debate on relativism. The debate, which continued through the 1940's, created much confusion, partly because Beard drew his arguments from Italian and German philosophers, notably Benedetto Croce, whose idealist epistemology he never really understood or shared. Ultimately, most historians decided that Beard went too far in denying objectivity and thereby made history too "present-minded." Yet his agitation left a lasting impact. It upset the complacent assumption of professional historians that moral judgment has no legitimate place in their work. It awakened a philosophical consciousness and renewed American receptivity to European historical theory.

Beard's death in 1948 coincided with a general reaction against his interpretation of American history. Much of the best scholarship since that time has gone to revise his stress on materialistic causation, on conflict rather than consensus, on the domestic rather than the international context of events. Attention has turned in good measure from interest groups to status groups and from rational to irrational motivation. Ironically, the history that Beard himself wrote in his old age prefigured this change of outlook: in the 1940's he put a new emphasis on ideas in history and on the role of individuals. He largely abandoned interpretation in economic terms. One characteristic that remained unaltered, however, was a lifelong rationalism, a determination to control power by reason.

# 8

---

# BEYOND CONSENSUS:
# THE HISTORIAN AS
# MORAL CRITIC

How, when, and to what extent do historians have a right to make explicit value judgments? The upheaval in American historiography after World War II put that hoary problem in a new perspective. Was the right (or privilege) of moral judgment impaired by the breakdown of the conceptual framework in which it had customarily functioned? Or might the exercise of such judgment now be improved? Could one find some guidance from the philosophers and the few European historians who were concurrently rethinking the problem of values in historical writing? My reflections on these questions were presented at a session of the American Historical Association in 1960 and printed in the American Historical Review, LXVII (Apr., 1962), 609–25.

Writing at the height of the conservative reaction against progressive history, I feared it would go too far. It did go too far, and we are now in the throes of an impetuous reaction against that reaction. But I was greatly mistaken in supposing that a complete loss of critical distance between historians and their America might develop. I have tempered my remarks on that point. Otherwise, the original essay remains unchanged.

*I*

A PERENNIAL DILEMMA of historical scholarship is its need to use the resources of the present to discover what is not present, but past. The creative historian lives a double life, responsive on one side to the questions and issues of his own age, faithful on the other side to the integrity of an age gone by. Too feeble an involvement in the life of the present makes for a slack and routine grasp of the past. But present commitments that are too parochial imprison our imagination, instead of challenging it. At one extreme, historical thought is sterile, at the other tendentious. How can historians, by the strength of their detachment, rise above a constricting present, and, by the amplitude of their commitment, enter a living past?

If this is a perennial problem, it has a special pertinence for the American academic historian. He works in a vast educational system that rewards its employees with prestige and security for predictable quantities of passionless research. The institutional setting, therefore, encourages much routine and mechanical history. On the other hand, the ideological conflicts of the twentieth century have swept many of our best historians in the opposite direction, entangling them in rather partisan commitments.

At times institutional restraints and ideological pressures have seemed to offset and balance one another in a fairly effective way. The pull of neutrality and the push of commitment maintained a tension that served the pursuit of truth. As long as our present concerns remained fundamentally stable, a cumulative pattern of research could be observed. Conventional monographs followed easily in paths marked out by the major interpretive studies, and confidence in the progress of knowledge kept criticism within manageable bounds. Now, however, that working balance has been upset. The old ideological positions have broken down, so that the kind of present-mindedness that seemed to illuminate American history in the 1940's has outlived its usefulness. Many of the values and allegiances that guided our historical writing now seem unduly restrictive. There is, consequently, a danger and an opportunity: the danger of a largely negative scholarship, revisionist in motive but routine or merely clever in result; the opportunity of discovering, with the help of our newer present, a history of unsuspected richness and power.

Until fairly recently, two contemporary commitments dominated the interpretation of American history. First, many of the best American historians felt a close identification with particular sections or social groups. Secondly, progressive and pragmatic ideas had an extraordinary control over historical thinking. Both of these circumstances have altered.

In an increasingly homogeneous society, historians are not likely to be as strongly motivated by sectional, class, and ethnic ties as many of them were a quarter of a century ago. Then militant southerners, confident westerners, defiant Brahmins, and the first self-conscious representatives of various ethnic minorities were turning up facets of our history reflective of their claims or grievances and championing regionalism, Puritanism, or cultural pluralism, as the case might be. Except in the area of Black history there is much less of this now. Scholars are not impelled to vindicate their respective social allegiances as ardently as Samuel Eliot Morison championed the Puritans, Walter Prescott Webb, the Great Plains, Carl Wittke, the immigrants, or Ulrich B. Phillips and E. Merton Coulter, the South.[1] One wonders how these various groupings in the American past will look to a new generation of historians, which is not anchored very securely in any of them.

While social changes were eroding the group loyalties of many historians, their generally progressive assumptions about American history were also breaking down. The two trends worked together. Just as progressive assumptions encouraged scholars to emphasize the struggle of contending groups in society, so the reaction against progressive historiography has discouraged such emphasis and has undermined the intellectual foundations of a group-centered point of view. We may, therefore, get to the heart of our current problem and opportunity when we understand what has happened to the progressive school of American historians.

From the American Revolution to the Second World War the great majority of our historians assumed that the underlying movement of American history was in the direction of improvement or betterment, not only in wealth but in freedom or happiness. In this movement, setbacks and even reverses had occurred, of course, when the American people were temporarily faithless to their basic principles. Such interludes were pronounced "Repressible Conflicts," "Great Aberrations," or "Great Betrayals,"[2] to indicate that they arose from mutual misunderstandings, irrational mistakes, and moral holidays, not from any fundamental defect in American culture. Even the fashionable disillusion of the 1920's left very little impress on professional historians. A President of the American Historical Association affirmed a law of progress in history in 1923, and in 1929 a leading authority on American social history urged his colleagues to synthesize their data by asking how every event or influence had checked or accelerated social evolution.[3] Attitudes such as these meant that historians were continually asking what each period "contributed" or "added" to the world of today. History was fundamentally aggregative. Even scholars devoted to the study of lost causes and vanished frontiers refused to draw pessimistic conclusions. They felt sure that the passing experience they cherished had left a permanent heritage of fruitful values.[4]

In the twentieth century these pervasive assumptions gave a strategic importance to historians who had a hardheaded explanation of the dynamics of change—historians who rendered the progressive faith realistically by explaining how and why human effort sometimes overcame human inertia and sometimes succumbed to it. Change, these scholars said, takes place through struggle, and progress occurs when the more popular and democratic forces overcome the resistance to change offered by vested interests. American history thus became a story of epic conflict between over- and underprivileged groups. Whether this strife was chiefly between sections, as with Frederick Jackson Turner, or between opposing economic groups, as with Charles Beard, or between Hamiltonian and Jeffersonian ideologies, as with Vernon Parrington, a fundamental dualism cut through the course of American history.[5]

In polarizing history vertically, the progressive realists also secured a principle of periodization. With eyes focused on the climactic moments in the continuing struggle, they dramatized the turning points when power had presumably shifted from one side to the other. Through revolution and counterrevolution, through reform and reaction, beat the rhythm of an exciting and meaningful history. Here indeed was a grand design, flexible, capacious, immediately relevant to the present interests of the 1920's and 1930's, capable of elaboration in a multitude of researches, yet very simple in outline. In 1939 Arthur Schlesinger, Sr., could compress a generation of historiography and the whole span of American political history into a single sentence: "A period of concern for the rights of the few has [regularly] been followed by one of concern for the wrongs of the many."[6]

Twenty years later, to most American historians, the grand design probably looked more like a grand illusion. Many of them in the 1950's had devoted their best energies to shattering the design. It had, without question, proved wanting. Too much of the mounting data of cultural, intellectual, and economic history overflowed the dialectical categories of liberal versus conservative. The groups to whom these labels were attached proved much less persistent and cohesive in identity and aim than the design allowed. The theory that change is effected through domestic social conflict took too little account of the role of accommodation and compromise in American political history, too little account of the kind of innovation emphasized in American business history, too little account of the international influences so important to diplomatic and intellectual history.

Yet the design might have held together after a fashion—by stretching and squeezing, it might have contained a good measure of new research—if the social attitudes that went into the design had remained intact. After World War II, however, historians found themselves in a new era, much less tractable and less responsive to progressive values. Some of those values now seemed too simple and too limited in their relevance to human experience. The vaunted realism of the progressive historians no longer seemed realistic enough.

As far as historians were concerned, one of the principal casualties of the postwar world was the faith in progress itself. Few of them became prophets of doom, but fewer still remained oracles of hope. Their disenchantment owed something to the powerful polemic of Reinhold Niebuhr but more to their own sharpened awareness of America's dependence on a precarious civilization. Walter Prescott Webb's *The Great Frontier* (Boston, 1952), although too extreme in its conclusions to win general acceptance, showed how an international perspective could cast a somber light on the epic theme of American progress: the frontier thesis became an explanation of the transitory, declining vitality of modern Western civilization. Other postprogressive scholars, such as George Kennan, studied American wars and diplomacy with an eye for the tragic and with a sense of the limits of American capacities.[7] The revisionist school of Civil War history declined when its thesis that partisan statesmen had willfully ignored constructive alternatives to a "needless" war and a "vindictive" peace began to look naïvely optimistic.[8]

Perhaps the most widespread effect of the sober postwar mood was to deflate progressive confidence in social change. Instead of endorsing change, or distinguishing between more or less desirable kinds, many historians grew cautious if not distrustful toward change as such. In the work of Ralph Gabriel, Clinton Rossiter, Louis Hartz, Daniel Boorstin, Robert E. Brown, Edmund Morgan, and others, a new appreciation of continuity in American history emerged. Neither in love with modernity nor entranced by the antique, many historians now emphasized the enduring uniformities of American life, the stability of institutions, the persistence of a national character.[9]

Thus, a conservative trend of historical interpretation set in, and as it gathered momentum it displayed other attitudes often found in conservative quarters. In contrast to the progressive historians' confidence in mass democracy, one notices among their immediate successors a skeptical attitude toward the common man and a reluctance to give full sympathy to the underdog. Such democratic heroes as Roger Williams, Nathaniel Bacon, Andrew Jackson, and Thorstein Veblen were now portrayed as less democratic or less heroic than earlier biographers had seen them.[10] On the other hand, such non-democratic figures as John Winthrop, Alexander Hamilton, Nicholas Biddle, George Fitzhugh, and John D. Rockefeller have risen several notches in historical reputation.[11]

This shift away from democratic affirmations should not be exaggerated. It did not, among many reputable historians, make heroes of the privileged and villains of their popular opponents. Such a reversal of progressive sympathies would preserve the progressive dichotomy between the many and the few, the haves and the have-nots. The deeper tendency in recent thought has been to dissolve the old polarities. Economic and ideological antitheses especially have blended together. Where the terms liberal and conservative remained in use, we found that liberal movements were after all conservative[12] and that almost all Americans have really been liberal.[13] Instead of the two-sided nation enshrined in progressive history—a nation eternally divided between a party of the past and a party of the future, between noble ideals and ignoble interests—the newer general interpretations showed us a single homogeneous culture, or perhaps a balanced interplay between three elements. The trinitarian approach lends itself neatly to a reconciliation of contrasts within a final synthesis.[14] Not conflict, therefore, but consensus was now taken as the normative reality of American life.

It is not hard to understand why this should be so. Unlike the progressive historian, his successor did not feel much at odds with powerful institutions or dominant social groups. He was not even half alienated. Carried along in the general postwar reconciliation between America and its intellectuals, and wanting to identify himself with a community, he usually read the national record for evidence of effective organization and a unifying spirit.[15]

Often the strength of this uniformitarian bent was obscured by the conservative or neo-liberal historian's delighted attention to the abundant variety of American life. Far from professing any love of conformity, he readily conceived of the American whole as an infinite number of freely related parts.[16] In his more critical moments, he might fear that the processes of centralization, bureaucratization, and standardization were going too far, and he embraced the variations and complexities in American experience all the more readily because they seemed to him so innocuous and impermanent. He discovered an immense variety of economic interests represented at Philadelphia in 1787, instead of only two. In restudying the Second Bank of the United States, Reconstruction, or the progressive movement, he fragmented into a welter of factions what the progressive historian had thought of as "the business community."[17] Immersed in fluid experience, he was often quite pragmatic in his antipathy to formal ideologies and clearly defined categories. His sense of the unity of America, therefore, was largely unspecific and rested on a description of its multiplicity. His motto might well have been *e pluribus unum*.

That this general approach to American history contains a large measure of truth, few will deny. Having much in common with our national mythology, it induced sympathies that were perhaps more general and less partisan than those of the progressive school. The historian of consensus was less immediately and urgently involved in the struggles of his own time; he might more easily project himself into the past on something like its own terms. The desire to see things whole, in the sense of understanding the working relationships between groups, has proved especially useful in the study of social history, which for too long was preoccupied with reform movements and social problems.

Moreover, the perception of external uniformities in American life stimulated intellectual history, for historians in search of drama turned to the subjective level of experience. A psychological approach to conflict enabled scholars to substitute a schism in the soul for a schism in society. Divisions, which a previous generation understood as basic opposition between distinct groups, acquired a more subtle meaning as psychological tensions running through the society as a whole.

On the whole the achievements of consensus historiography have been substantial, and the ferment of reinterpretation has given a fine zest to the study of American history. Yet the kind of judgment that the new historiography makes of the national record cannot go unquestioned. Insofar as simplicity has yielded to complexity, our perception of the lessons history can teach may be enriched. Insofar as consensus gives an even simpler view of American history than we had before, it threatens critical judgment. Fortunately, the recognition of consensus in the past has not usually been unqualified. Nor has it always been presumed to sanction the status quo. Of the outstanding books of the 1950's some retained a modified progressive outlook, like C. Vann Woodward's *Origins of the New South, 1877–1913* (1951). Some expressed a disillusioned liberalism, like Richard Hofstadter's *The Age of Reform: From Bryan to F. D. R.* (1955) and Henry Nash Smith's *Virgin Land: The American West as Symbol and Myth* (1950). In many ways, however, the emphasis on consensus and continuity softened the outlines and flattened the crises of American history. A certain tameness and amiability crept into our view of things. In functioning as a conservative frame of reference, the consensus approach gave us a bland history, in which conflict was muted, in which the classic issues of social justice were underplayed, in which the elements of spontaneity, effervescence, and violence in American life got little sympathy or attention. As the progressive impulse subsided, scholarship was threatened with moral complacency, parading often in the guise of neutrality.

## II

To speak of moral complacency or neutrality is to raise afresh an old question that too many of us have regarded as long since settled. Since the rise of scientific history, the legitimacy of moral judgments in historical writing has been under official disapproval. By the end of the nineteenth century, the manuals of historical method had summarily banished moral evaluation from the proper sphere of historical science; recent handbooks continue to ignore it.[18] But the present situation has reopened this question. From English and

German scholars we hear warnings that academic history, by shrinking from evaluations of right and wrong, has helped to weaken the spirit of personal responsibility.[19] The warning has a special application to American historiography. With the decline of progressive values, the principal moral energy on which American historians have drawn in the twentieth century became less available. There is no substitute in the dubious affirmations of consensus. Yet the contemporary situation offers a third alternative. We have a major opportunity for revitalizing the moral relevance of historical scholarship.

Until history became professionalized, its practitioners felt no misgivings about teaching moral lessons. History, to them, exhibited universal laws of human nature and so comprised a vast repository of political and moral example. The nineteenth century faith in progress put a supreme confidence into such moralizing; for the historian's assumption that he stood at the summit of history, and could therefore truly judge the actions and standards of earlier times by those of his own, expunged any doubt about his moral authority. He might exercise it with advantage in any field of history, although the study of one's own country was particularly improving. "That study," said the president of Harvard University in 1884, summing up a common conviction,

shows the young the springs of public honor and dishonor; sets before them the national failings, weaknesses, and sins; warns them against future dangers by exhibiting the losses and sufferings of the past; enshrines in their hearts the national heroes; and strengthens in them the precious love of country.[20]

The same year in which Charles W. Eliot spoke, the American Historical Association was established by men who were retreating from moral commitment in the name of science. The scientific historian aspired to be a flawless mirror reflecting an independent, external reality. By freely pronouncing judgments he would distort the picture. Yet the scientific historians, in denying themselves a judicial function, did not intend to lessen history's didactic usefulness. Secure in their faith in progress, they commonly supposed that objective history would reveal the evolution of morality in the march of events without intrusive comment by the writer.[21] Surely, over the long run, history displayed the gradual advance of wisdom and virtue. If the historian took care of the facts, the values would take care of themselves. In practice, of course, the early professional historians could not suppress moral rhetoric completely. But they could in principle forswear it without any sense of risk or anxiety, since scientific history emerged in America in a humane milieu, unperplexed by deep frustrations.

The new style progressives of the twentieth century, rebelling against the conservative implications of scientific history, were less complacent. They were activists, whose expectations of progress depended on the use of historical knowledge in order to control history. They felt less comfortable about the present than their conservative predecessors had, and they determined to link the past to current needs for reform.[22] They recognized a legitimate place for values in historical interpretation. By renouncing an unattainable objectivity, they hoped to arrive at usable truths.

In progressive hands American history became not only a struggle between the many and the few but a realm of clashing values. Once more, the American historian consciously played the role of moral critic, now with a pragmatic emphasis on the consequences of policies and ideas, instead of the easy dogmatism of a George Bancroft or a Francis Parkman. Unfortunately, however, the restoration of moral urgency in historical scholarship occurred on too narrow a front and too precarious a basis. The same progressive spirit that stirred the heart and conscience of historians also, in other aspects, severely limited their moral vision. For one thing, the range of moral concern contracted from the whole life of man to certain political and economic issues. The progressive historian did not ordinarily search the past for light on personal codes of behavior, the great sphere of private as opposed to public morality. Nor did he show much interest in studying the resolution of incompatible loyalties, or the nature of responsibility, greatness, initiative, and the like. His view of history remained largely impersonal: he concentrated on "social forces" as the earlier scientific historians had concentrated on "institutions." The only kind of ethics that engaged the progressive historian's interest was the ethics of democracy,[23] and even here he was pretty exclusively concerned with the actualization of democratic values rather than their relation to other goods.

This tendency to dwell on means rather than ends—on the attainable results of an ideal rather than its intrinsic nature—reflected the progressive scholar's reluctance to venture much beyond the accustomed limits of scientific objectivity. He wanted his values, but he wanted them in the shape of facts. Tough-minded, realistic, disdainful of nineteenth century pieties and platitudes, he tried to be pragmatic in his moral judgments. The practical results of any historical situation—the tangible action it produced—dominated and restricted his evaluation of it. Progressive historians ordinarily retained too much confidence in progress to doubt that the course of history would vindicate their democratic and pragmatic ethics.[24]

From these antecedents have come many of the "consensus" historians of today. While reacting against a reformist bias, some of them continue to measure the past by pragmatic standards. What remains for them of the moral function of the historian now that the inspiration of social progress has dimmed, and the age of reform that lasted for half a century has passed? When stability rather than change became the national objective, what values could pass the pragmatic test? Only what was snugly enmeshed in the texture of American experience had clearly proved its practical worth. Deprived of an active commitment to progress, the pragmatic approach tended to endorse sheer success and survival. Having lost its critical edge, pragmatism could deteriorate into restrospective piety.

On the other hand, the present situation can give rise to a very different kind of historical scholarship, a scholarship engaged in a more widely ranging and a subtler moral criticism than American professional historians have yet undertaken. A lively critical impulse has clearly survived in many quarters. It is seeking a new field of expression now that the grand design of progressive historiography no longer contains and directs it. That impulse can draw today on a richer knowledge of human motivation than scholars have ever had at their disposal before; it can achieve a sympathetic under-

standing of a greater variety of human types. Having learned something of the relativity of values, historians can exercise a morally
critical function with tentativeness and humility, with a minimum
of self-righteousness, and with a willingness to meet the past on
equal terms.

How can this come about? Let us look first at the pitfalls to be
avoided; here the record of American historiography to date can
guide us. None of the formal postures that American historians have
conventionally adopted seem adequate any longer, either morally or
historically. Neither the dogmatic moralist, nor the pure scientist,
nor the pragmatist offers a satisfactory model.

Surely scholars may not, without corrupting history, revert to the
judicial stance of a century ago. We are now too well aware of the
wide disparities between ethical systems, and too ignorant of their
relation to one another, to impose our own arbitrarily on another
time and place. Let us beware of the easy temptations of moral judgment in essaying the difficult adventure of moral criticism. Let us
operate on any subject with a conviction of its dignity and worth.
Let us grant to every actor in a historical drama the fullest measure
of his particular integrity; let us not destroy the drama by hastening
to condemn or to absolve. The serious historian may not wrap himself in judicial robes and pass sentence from on high; he is too much
involved in both the prosecution and the defense. He is not a judge
of the dead, but rather a participant in their affairs, and their only
trustworthy intermediary.

For these tasks, the moral neutrality of the scientific position has
likewise proved wanting. In addition to the standard complaints—
that it is unattainable, that it dehumanizes history, that it encourages fatalism and gives us nothing to admire—one may suggest a
further difficulty. Scientific history, so far as it achieves neutrality,
leaves an unbridged gulf between the subject and the reader. The
scientific historian, in liberating his readers from moral absolutism,
apparently assumed that they could make their own fair and independent judgments if given an unobstructed view of the past. On
principle, therefore, the scientific historian did not address himself
to the sensibilities of a particular audience. He did not deliberately

connect its needs and perplexities with those of another time and place. Indeed, he was scarcely conscious of having an audience. Whereas the historical judge coerced the reader, the historical scientist ignored him. To write as a critic, however, is to assume an active responsibility both to a phase of the past and to a contemporary public, and to engage one with the other.

Our third model—the historical pragmatist—more nearly approximates that kind of role. He is very much aware of present needs, and his pronouncements are tentative and undogmatic. But his sympathies are limited, and his criticism does not go deep. Criteria that rest on a program of practical action take account of a restricted present as well as a restricted past. A morality confined to social engineering emphasizes results at the expense of intentions. In a progressive age, it becomes a partisan in the struggle for results. In a conservative age, it celebrates results already largely achieved.

Once the pragmatic test is suspended, historians will still analyze the results of a situation in order to discover its causes and to learn how those particular results came to be; but a moral appraisal of the situation need not depend upon its outcome. A truly sensitive critic will go beyond the practical consequences of the process he describes. He may criticize his subject, not on the ground of its present relevance, but for its intrinsic value as a gesture of the human spirit.

One may well ask, however, for more specific directions. What strategies can the historian legitimately employ without compromising the integrity of his craft? What criteria may he apply in performing the office of moral critic? How much real change in historical scholarship is implied? These questions lead us into an aspect of historiography ignored by the standard manuals and treatises on method. Discussion has not ordinarily gone beyond the point of recognizing that the historian's own values inevitably color his writing. At best, we have acknowledged this coloring as a mark of our humanity.[25] Professional historians have hardly begun to consider moral insight as something they can gain by skilled and patient historical study, not merely as something they cannot keep out of it. Historical method acquires a new dimension when we begin to speak of the criticism of life in addition to the technical criticism of documents. Then moral evaluation becomes a professional task, not just a predilection of our unprofessional selves.

A comparison with analogous developments in literary studies during the last generation may help to clarify the opportunity in historical scholarship. The reign of the literary historian—exclusively preoccupied with historical and biographical backgrounds to literature, with sources, influences, and social conditions—was challenged by the incursion of literary critics into academic circles.[26] Various schools of literary criticism proliferated, but all subordinated factual description and historical explanation to a close evaluation of the work of art. For a time, criticism went to absurdly antihistorical extremes. English departments split into factions—literary historians versus New Critics. But the ferment invigorated literary history enormously; in the hands of men like F. O. Matthiessen, Lionel Trilling, and Harry Levin, the study of literature profited from the interplay of critical and historical perspectives.

Possibly the professional study of history would benefit at least as much from the challenge of a similar movement, directed at the criticism of life rather than the criticism of art. On this analogy, we may look forward to something more noteworthy than the recent fruitless debate over the legitimacy of those present-centered judgments that inescapably condition all historical knowledge. Instead, we may look forward to the development of a partial distinction between the kind of historical inquiry that is familiar and traditional and a newer kind that is only beginning to appear in professional circles. The older type aims chiefly at knowledge of causal relationships in a particular phase of the past; the newer type aims chiefly at knowledge of the elements of good and evil discoverable in a particular historical setting. The former type holds moral appraisal in check in the interest of causal synthesis. The latter type, with equal propriety, subordinates causal interpretation to moral interpretation. Both endeavors will inevitably reflect the historian's own commitments. Both must accept the distinctively historical obligation to deal with a whole situation in its authentic complexity. But causal history should have a form appropriate to the actual *course* of experience; whereas moral history, proceeding with a similar drive for discovery, will take whatever shape seems best suited to elaborate the problematical *qualities* of experience.

This distinction, like any classification of historical studies, should not be pressed too far, though it can serve some useful purposes. It calls attention to the need for a thoroughgoing moral criticism, in contrast to the impressionistic moral judgments that creep into historical writing at every turn. A working distinction between causal history and moral history also guards against pragmatic confusion between facts and values. Moreover, it helps to equalize the legitimacy and importance of two great objectives: the reconstruction of history as objective reality (most appropriate to causal history), and the participation in history as subjective experience (essential to moral history).[27] Causal history and moral history at their best, however, are reciprocal modes of understanding, each of which suffers from neglect of the other. Let us distinguish between them as friendly rivals in order to overcome a destructive enmity.

A closer look at the nature of moral history will suggest how it can supplement and enrich existing scholarship. One may discern, within the wide domain of moral history, two general types. The first type deals with the whole quality of a life, a complex of lives, or an age. It enables us to grasp the moral tone of a particular time and place—to feel the involuntary drift and pressure of its values against a background of alternatives delivered in other times and places. How has the notion of honor changed since the Middle Ages? What did men mean in the nineteenth century when they spoke of "character" and put implicit confidence in leaders or associates who had it? To what sorts of people did the virtue of "character" appeal and attach? What tangled combinations of courage and weakness, or of love and hate, do we find pervading a career, a movement, or a period? Similarly, moral insight may reveal fundamental polarities in history that are more illuminating than class or sectional divisions. Is the great cleavage in American history the outward one between haves and have-nots, which twentieth century progressives observed in society, or is it rather an inward opposition, which progressives strove to reconcile within themselves, between an ethic of communal responsibility and an ethic unrestrained individualism?

These questions point to an extended kind of moral history that shades imperceptibly into causal history, and differs only in having somewhat more interest in the intrinsic meaning of the experience and somewhat less in explaining its development. Professional historians seem to be venturing increasingly into this genre, though more readily in casual essays than in their formal, full-dress works. Carl Becker was probably the first American professional historian to become adept at an intellectualized moral history, which may help to account for his great and continuing vogue in recent years. It remains true, however, that the major works of this kind are still written mostly by literary and cultural critics like Wilbur J. Cash, Hannah Arendt, and Lewis Mumford.[28] The amateur in history plunges instinctively and often rashly into moral criticism. A quickened interest among professional scholars would surely help academic history to find its rightful place in the republic of letters.

A second kind of moral history concentrates on particular acts of choice. Here we confront not involuntary or cumulative processes, but rather the moments of important human initiative, and we ponder the moral responsibility of the agents of decision. In the 1760's the British Parliament adopted a disastrous policy of spasmodic coercion toward the American colonies. A generation ago American scholars debated the constitutionality of that policy, and British scholars are still arguing about the exact nature of English government at the time;[29] but the momentous decision that precipitated the American Revolution has not yet had close attention as a problem in political ethics. Given the political and social institutions of the day, what real alternatives were present? Who erred most culpably? What balance of folly, insight, and constructive purpose can we discern in each of the major participants?[30] The study of moral responsibility remains crude unless each of the elements contributory to a situation fully exhibits its distinctive abilities, limitations, and dilemmas. Ideally, each element should effect a criticism of the others. As the author's design unfolds, the situation becomes luminous with unexpected contingencies.

In similar fashion it should be possible to study afresh the turning points in the lives of well-known individuals: Robert E. Lee's painful decision to cast his lot with the Confederacy in 1861, William James's famous affirmation of free will in 1870, Franklin D. Roosevelt's acceptance of a third term in 1940. Seizing upon the event, the historian can undertake to clarify the degree and quality of initiative suggested by a close comparison with other individuals similarly circumstanced (James with Henry Adams, for example). History becomes a meditation on the choices that might conceivably have been made, as well as those that were.

In all such studies of an act of decision, as in larger studies of the moral climate, criticism cannot do without some causal analysis. We hold people responsible only to the degree that we think them free to choose their own course. The imaginable range of choice within a particular situation guides our moral criticism, which must therefore include an appreciation of the unalterable conditions that bulk large in causal history. Yet moral criticism not only borrows from causal analysis, but also contributes to it. By enlarging our awareness of the latent possibilities of a situation, criticism will suggest new causal hypotheses. Perhaps it would be better to speak, not of causal history and moral history as separate types, but of two kinds of attention, each of which contributes to historical wisdom.

There remains the difficult question of the criteria that the critic of the past may legitimately employ. Surely one must have standards. Just as surely, the only proper standards are ones common to the historian and to the world he is studying. But to try to lay down exact criteria is, I think, to misconceive our opportunity and to narrow our prospect. The historian is not called to establish a hierarchy of values, but rather to explore a spectrum of human potentialities and achievements. While maintaining his own integrity, while preserving the detachment that time and distance afford, he must participate in variety, allowing his subjects as much as possible to criticize one another. In fact, the obligation of the historian to become a moral critic grows out of the breakdown of ethical absolutes. If no single ethical system, even a pragmatic one that trusts the piecemeal results of history, does justice to all situations, a complex awareness must take the place of systematic theory. Instead of depending on fixed canons or rules, the moral critic must learn from the great dramatists like Shakespeare, from novelists like Tolstoy, and from the matchless example of Thucydides.

In the simplest sense, the historian commits to moral criticism all the resources of his human condition. He derives from moral criticism an enlarged and disciplined sensitivity to what men ought to have done, what they might have done, and what they achieved. His history becomes an intensive, concrete reflection upon life, freed from academic primness, and offering itself as one of the noblest, if also one of the most difficult and imperfect, of the arts.

This discussion, instead of continuing the current argument about the interpretation of American history, has turned outward toward a wider horizon. But perhaps the original issue has undergone a partial resolution. When the historian's quest for understanding reaches beyond pragmatic and empirical concerns, he need not strain to find patterns of conflict or of consensus. He will have plenty of both. He will study, as the most meaningful kind of consensus, the moral standards of an age—what, distinctively, it assumed about the conduct of life. He will find conflict wherever those moral standards clash or break down, and so force men to make a choice. In confronting all that is unstable and precarious in human values, he can discover the profoundest struggles and conflicts that the drama of history affords.

# 9

---

# AMERICAN

# HISTORIOGRAPHY

# IN THE 1960's

A SHORTER VERSION *of this paper was written specifically for a two-day symposium at the University of Wisconsin in April, 1968, in honor of Merle Curti on the occasion of his retirement. It appears here in print for the first time.*

*The judgments ventured in this lecture cannot pass for much more than tentative impressions of desultory reading. In writing the lecture I was slipping back temporarily into the occupational narcissism of the historiographer, from which I had resolved to disengage myself. I was therefore limited to what could be said without benefit of sustained or systematic study. Doubtless the personal tone those circumstances dictated is well to preserve in dealing with so current a topic.*

FIVE YEARS HAVE PASSED since I put the finishing touches on a book that purported to trace the course of American historical scholarship from the nineteenth century to the present. [1] Five years are not, by the usual reckoning of historians, a very long time. It is certainly not long enough to permit a thorough reconsideration of one's conclusions. Yet those few years are more than sufficient to provoke some anxious afterthoughts. They are more than enough to give rise to uneasy second thoughts about the projections made in that book and the judgments offered there about the contemporary historical world. The intellectual situation I took as contemporary was approximately that of 1960. The overall view I gave of trends in scholarship had formed in my mind as a result of the extraordinary upheaval that occurred during the 1950's in the interpretation of American history. Now we do not yet stand at a decade's remove from that point of observation, but we are at least in the latter part of the 1960's, and it should be possible to ask wherein the scholarship of the sixties is fulfilling my expectations and wherein it is not.

First a word should be said about the overall tone of my conclusions five years ago. They were consistently, indeed determinedly, cheerful. I knew that the evidence I had assembled gave no unambiguous grounds for optimism. I knew that the same evidence might be read as foretelling a different set of consequences. But my own circumstances were such that I could not escape being hopeful about the future of the profession I had come to love. I had recently joined at a great university a department undergoing an exciting intellectual revival. Its vigor seemed to me in some measure representative of what was occurring throughout American higher education as the increasing rewards of academic life and the post-Sputnik demand for intellectual achievement quickened the pace and raised the standard of performance all along the line.

But how much was history, and specifically the writing of American history, likely to benefit from conditions that might merely feed the self-esteem of a mandarin class? Was I unconsciously slipping into the role (hideous thought!) of apologist for the mandarins? Was I, to be more charitable, too easily supposing that the mere application of a rich manure to the gardens of American scholarship would yield the particular cultural flowers, the great works of history, I wanted to see? All this worried me. Extended reflection on what was actually happening in the interpretation of American history tended, however, to relieve my fears. The problems that had concerned me deeply in the late 1950's seemed in the early 1960's to be moving toward a promising (though still indistinct) resolution. The seedbed of American historical studies wore, I thought, the signs of an approaching spring.

The chief obstacle to the full development of the field, I believed in the late 1950's, was conceptual. Our historical writing was becoming imbued with the Tocquevillean idea that all Americans are basically alike. The emphasis on consensus in American history, though it had the merit of destroying an older stereotype, seemed to create a new one that was at least as false and considerably more vacuous from a moral point of view. It was false especially to the effervescence, the explosive conflicts, the discontinuities in our history. The idea of an American consensus enabled us to take seriously the concept of national character, which had been unjustly denigrated for several decades. Too commonly, however, national character was now adopted as a framework rather than a variable, as a unifying principle rather than a problem. Did not the stress on homogeneity and continuity undercut interest in the dimension of change, and was this not an offense against the historical sense itself?

These dire anticipations were punctured by two surprises. First, my early polemical outbursts against the "consensus" school of historians[2] were received with widespread applause and very little criticism. This might, of course, be taken as a mark of obtuseness, or it might reflect a very devious form of consensualism—an unwillingness to be drawn into any controversy at all. But my own conclusion on being so widely praised was that the tendency I complained of must not be so far advanced or deeply entrenched as I had imagined. After attacking the so-called consensus historians at an annual meeting several years ago, I was shaken to receive from an elderly lady a letter thanking me for disclosing the real nature of the conspiracy that had caused her manuscript to be rejected by so many university presses. She implored me to help her find a press that was not under the control of the new school.

Meanwhile my book was progressing. I was trying to pack the whole corpus of historiography into the interpretive framework my preconceptions had erected. As data accumulated, more and more of it would not fit. Distinctions between today's consensus historians and their progressive predecessors were not nearly as sharp as I had believed. In fact, I discovered that the trend I had perceived so suddenly in the 1950's as a major movement had really originated in the 1930's. It stemmed from a crisis within progressive thought, not from an assault from outside the pale. Moreover, the significant changes since World War II seemed less and less the possession of an identifiable group. They were in the air. They affected everyone but in different degrees and ways. There was indeed too much stress on consensus among some leading writers, but American historical thought had not congealed into distinct schools. Instead, it was swirling around a few central problems. Evidently I had underestimated both the degree of continuity and the range of diversity in our historiography. Was not the prospect before us much more cheering than I had supposed?

This, in a general way, was the ground of my optimism. Whether or not it was merited I am not yet in a position to say. Let us, however, descend to a lower level of generality and consider the more specific projections I made within this generally attractive outlook. Of the particular avenues of progress that I envisioned, how many are we actually traversing?

As far as American history is concerned, I suggested that three emergent trends might be expected to prosper. First, there was a new institutionalism which had begun to materialize in the 1950's and was yielding its first fruits in books like Alfred Chandler's *Strategy and Structure,* the Stanley Elkins and Eric McKitrick studies of slavery and Reconstruction, and Richard McCormick's research on voting patterns.[3] These historians explained behavior in terms of the functional requirements of organized systems. They manifested a growing interest in a kind of history that locates men within structures which define their roles and shape their behavior. Second, I thought there were strong indications that an international and comparative approach to American history would make rapid progress, partly along the lines suggested by Frank Thistlethwaite's fine book, *The Anglo-American Connection,* and partly in the sociological direction pointed out by Frank Tannenbaum and David M. Potter.[4] Third, I ventured to say that moral criticism in historical writing was likely to become richer, more illuminating, more deeply human. An increasing psychological awareness should equip morally engaged historians to write about the dilemmas of others with feeling as well as understanding.[5]

These exciting developments in American history might also, of course, prove their worth in other areas of historical study; I did not know enough about other areas to hazard an opinion on the strength of such trends. Still, I thought I knew the temper and the tasks of the whole profession well enough to anticipate two advances of a somewhat general kind. I contended that the rancorous quarrels over methodology and philosophy, which had tended to polarize historians during the thirties and forties, were giving way to a sophisticated fusion of science and art. I predicted, in short, a convergence of warring methodologies. And, partly for that reason, I believed that historians were regaining a capacity to reach a wider adult audience —not a general audience to be sure, but a literate audience of non-specialists.[6]

Such were the anticipations with which I faced the 1960's. Three of them had to do with the trend of research in American history, the other two with the performance of the profession at large. How reliable do these predictions sound today?

In announcing the emergence of a new institutional history I seem to have made no mistake. This is becoming one of the most vigorous aspects of American historiography. In effect, historians have begun thinking (as well as acting) on a simple sociological principle. People are identified and defined by the social systems within which they work and live. They respond more directly to the demands of the system than they do to a larger, more miscellaneous "environment." Therefore, historians should pay more attention to social structures and less to environments. This institutional history differs significantly from the kind that flourished in the late nineteenth century. It looks for organizational patterns not primarily in legal frameworks but in the informal arrangement of power. Thus constitutional history has not enjoyed any notable revival, though its most illustrious practitioners (like the University of Wisconsin's Willard Hurst) have interests that are very similar to those of the new institutionalists.[7] The latter seem to say, in effect, that a vast disintegration and reconstitution of authority may form the central theme of American history. It is symptomatic that the first general synthesis of a period in American history written from an institutional point of view should be entitled *The Search for Order*.[8]

On a monographic level, institutional historians have found an especially congenial subject in the study of political parties. Perhaps I should say in the study of the party system; for one of the key concepts in the recent literature is a distinction between the first and the second party systems, and it is characteristic now to see parties at any given time as symbiotically related to one another. Thus, David Fischer in a monograph on the contribution of the Federalist party to the democratization of American politics (a topic that would in itself have been inconceivable a mere twelve or fifteen years ago) writes: "The agency of change was not the action of one party but the interaction of two."[9]

A grand inquest is underway into the social and cultural bases of the major parties, their electoral habits, and their influence on foreign policy. But a systemic approach to American politics has now been carried beyond the party structure itself in James Sterling Young's elegant book, *The Washington Community, 1800–1828*.[10] Here for the first time the subject of study is the whole cluster of legislative and executive personnel assembled in Washington. In their ways of living and working together we perceive more clearly than ever before the basic political problems of the new nation. The feebleness of party organization, together with the many consequences of that fact, is revealed more fully than would be possible in any book confined to the history of parties. No more important a contribution to American institutional history has been published in the last five years.

The fact that Young belongs to the fraternity of political scientists rather than historians and the additional fact that he makes good use of statistical techniques like the Rice Index of Cohesion suggest how heavily the new institutionalism draws on contemporary social sciences. Indeed, one of its sources of strength is a reawakening interest in historical data on the part of social scientists, and one of its prime attractions to young historians is the opportunity it offers for analytic precision. Both the conceptual rigor and the quantitative methods that are valued by social scientists are contributing importantly to the revival of institutional history. The description of institutionalized behavior conduces to a certain amount of abstraction, and this in turn permits the formulation of alternative hypotheses suitable for statistical verification. By counting roll calls or plotting locations on a map, the institutional historian can try to isolate distinct variables and secure, on however modest a scale, some "hard" results.

The institutional approach has spread into many fields other than political history. It is engendering a lively interest in the history of the professions, as the studies of Daniel H. Calhoun and others demonstrate.[11] It is opening the history of one of the most important and most neglected of all institutions, the family.[12] It is revitalizing American urban history. Or perhaps I should say, more accurately, that the history of town and city is being transformed into the history of the community conceived as a functioning whole. Of this undertaking, recent studies of Boston by Darrett Rutman and Roger Lane, and an important analysis of Philadelphia by Sam B. Warner, Jr., are good examples.[13]

In spite of the importance of statistical series in most of the books I have mentioned, it would be a mistake to suppose that institutional history is entirely complementary to and dependent upon the new quantitative techniques that some historians are fervently espousing. A fine enthusiasm for the methods that characterize what is proudly called "the new economic history" and the "new political history" has become a challenging and fruitful part of the life of our discipline.[14] This is a development that will bear looking at for its own import. As far as institutional history is concerned, it cuts two ways. Although quantification encourages the study of recurrent (i.e., institutionalized) behavior, it also tempts a devotee to neglect the relationships he cannot measure. To be rigorous, he has to abstract a very few variables from the total context in which they functioned. In economic history—the field in which the new methods have been most highly developed—the difficulty of combining statistical finesse with the historical synthesis essential to the study of institutions has become fully apparent; "cliometricians" and institutionalists have parted company. [15] An institutional historian will be well served by the new methods if he can take them or leave them, if he can apply them at a few critical points without shattering his sense of structure or limiting his capacity to evaluate the unmeasurable. Quantification can easily fragment the institutional vision of human behavior.

Actually, some of the best institutional history now being written rests almost wholly on traditional historical research. A particular objective of the new institutionalists is to grasp the purposes that induced men to combine in the way they did rather than some other way, and so to perceive the human aims (often diverse and clashing) that the institution served. This kind of inquiry engenders a new affinity between institutional and intellectual history, such that some of the most interesting intellectual history being written today is equally a contribution to the history of institutions. Thus Edmund S. Morgan's delightful little book, *Visible Saints,* explores a crucial theological dilemma as it became manifest in the adoption and revision of a particular criterion for church membership. Gordon Wood has brought an extraordinary understanding of political and social thought to bear on the constitutional system created in the 1770's and 1780's.[16] These are time-honored topics that acquire a new coherence through the inter-penetration of institutions and ideas.

Closely associated with the institutional is the comparative approach to American history. In effect, one supplies a context for the other, for institutions (and of course ideas as well) assume an otherwise unattainable clarity and significance when observed in more than one historical setting or in a setting large enough to display the effect of varying conditions. Both the institutional and the comparative approach call for a highly developed sense of structure; so it is not surprising to find the two approaches joined in a good many of the best books of the 1960's: in Louis Hartz's *The Founding of New Societies* and Seymour Lipset's *The First New Nation;* in Jack Pole's *Political Representation in England and the Origins of the American Republic*; in various writings by Bernard Bailyn and Felix Gilbert; and in the extraordinary new scholarship on slavery that is coming particularly from Eugene Genovese and David B. Davis.[17]

What is surprising about comparative history is not that it should at last have begun to flourish but that its flourishing should have been so long delayed. Why were our historians so slow to respond to the challenge of Marc Bloch and Max Weber? Why did they fail to follow up the international perspectives in the early work of Marcus Hansen, Richard Shryock, Howard Mumford Jones, and Merle Curti, all of whom acquired in the era of the First World War an understanding of America's continuous participation in a larger cultural community?[18] Why in the next generation did that view of American history deteriorate so badly that we have even yet hardly begun to capitalize fully on the opportunities for comparative study created after World War II by the Fulbright and other international programs? One possible answer lies in the arduous pursuit of interdisciplinary wisdom that characterized the 1930's and 1940's. Like the dominant American school of anthropologists, many historians tried so hard to grasp the intersection of various types of experience within a single society that the effort to be interdisciplinary got in the way of being intercultural. Surely this was one consequence of the American Studies movement, which tended to envelop us in the many-layered texture of our own national experience instead of posing distinctively historical problems in a comparative context.

The American Studies movement gave much encouragement to one concept that was at least implicitly comparative, the concept of national character. This was, as I have suggested, an analytic tool of the consensus history of the 1950's and the basis for its major achievements. One cannot, of course, discuss national traits without pondering national differences, so historians in the 1950's found themselves inevitably involved more and more in comparisons. Yet the interest of the consensus historians centered so exclusively on the differences between the United States and Europe that they only prepared the way for a more explicit, fully developed kind of comparative study. That has come in the 1960's with the decline of the idea of consensus, a loosening of the restrictive embrace of the concept of national character, and a more careful, more systematic effort to identify differences within a context of similarities. In all those respects the comparative approach to American history really came of age in the work of a Europeanist looking at the United States from the outside, i.e., Robert Palmer's *Age of the Democratic Revolution*.[19] Unlike Palmer, most students of American history continue to think of the comparative approach primarily as a device for bringing out distinctive features of the United States. But it is a measure of the distance we have come in a decade that we now have from a scholar trained in American history an imaginative study of a common political culture operating in Britain, Canada, and the United States in the late nineteenth century.[20]

Thus two of my prognostications have so far proved close to the mark. On the third point, a rise in moral criticism, my understanding of contemporary trends may now seem to have been less sure. The subject is full of perplexity, and the ground we might like to stake out is shifting beneath our feet. Although nothing can be said on this subject with confidence, I now think that moral criticism in American historiography is becoming both more pronounced and less perceptive than I had supposed it might be.

For a long time American historiography, with its strong progressive tradition, has been shaped by instrumental considerations, which have kept us keenly aware of interrelations between past and present. Americans, as J. R. Pole recently observed, lack "that sense, inescapable in Europe, of the total, crumbled irrecoverability of the past, of its differentness, of the fact that it is dead."[21] Most of us do not completely accept the touch of censure in Pole's observation. Most of us like to think of the past as living still in the present. That is why it seemed to me desirable, if not likely, that the moral involvement formerly contained in progressive history should not subside but should instead secure a more flexible expression in our postprogressive era through an enlarged capacity on the part of historians to participate sympathetically in the value conflicts and moral choices men have wrestled with in the past.

Neither my concern over a possible decline in moral commitment nor my hope for a more fluent exercise of it is proving to be very well founded. I failed utterly to anticipate the spread during the

last five years of a new radicalism, which has given suddenly a
terrible passion and urgency to the criticism of American culture.
How short a while ago it was that the Kennedy administration
seemed to seal the reconciliation between America and its intellectuals, while those who remained at all disaffected bewailed the
absence of effective social criticism! Yet today I have the impression
that the number of scholarly histories born of protest or alienation,
and explicitly intended to relate the struggles of the past to the
needs of the present, is rapidly increasing. The best example is the
flood of books on Negro-white relations, especially the new literature
on Reconstruction and the reappraisal of the abolitionists. Characteristically, a recent book edited by Martin Duberman concludes
with an essay comparing the abolitionists' tactics with those of the
freedom riders of the 1960's. An equally fervent identification with
another tradition of protest appears in Alan Heimert's massive
work, *Religion and the American Mind.*[22] To judge from the restless temper of many of the best graduate students one encounters
these days, an explicit search for a relevant past is likely to become
still more widespread and ardent in the next few years.

In professional journals and meetings the current intensification
of moral commitment among historians has been received with
remarkable indulgence. This accomodating attitude seems to derive
partly from a widespread malaise, a general sense that our society is
indeed sick and that its illness has not been fully diagnosed. Partly
also radical historians have been sustained by a common American
tendency to associate boldness and energy with innovation. It is
commonly assumed that radical criticism of American society is
almost bound to yield valuable new interpretations of American
history.[23] The record to date gives that assumption little support.
The New Left does include some of the best of the younger historians, and through the writings of Eugene Genovese and Gabriel
Kolko it has contributed significantly to the flourishing analysis of
social structure, which also engages many historians with more
moderate views.[24] As a group, however, the radical scholars have
found no consistent or distinctive approach to American history.
Their books and articles have very little in common except a hos-

tility to liberalism. Their predominant cast of mind—deeply suspicious of all powerful institutions and ruling elites—is illuminating the failures and rigidities in American policies. But this kind of mind generally has little patience for the weighing of historical alternatives. Consequently it has tended to be casual or superficial in accounting for social change.

Radical scholarship appears most effective when it is most austere and clinical. In a time of turmoil like the present, historians who deal in praise and blame are in danger of sounding shrill. Of a major scholarly movement that claims the function of moral judgment we are entitled to ask for a widening, not a mere reversal, of perspectives; an enrichment of our humanity, not a mere confirmation of our likes and dislikes. This in turn calls for a certain charity: a blend of sympathy and distance, a combination of empathic identification with analytic detachment. That sort of historical writing remains as rare today as it has always been in the United States. Yet its possibilities are suggested on a small scale in Willie Lee Rose's *Rehearsal for Reconstruction* and on a larger scale in Bernard Bailyn's *Ideological Origins of the American Revolution*.[25] Although Mrs. Rose's exquisite miniature is a narrative of people while Professor Bailyn's robust mural is an analysis of ideas, both books delve into men's motives and decisions in a way that permits us simultaneously to judge and to understand.

If it is true that humane appraisals in the manner of Rose and Bailyn are in short supply relative to the other types of historical effort I have been discussing, there would appear to be a certain disequilibrium in the present capacities of American historians. Moral criticism flounders, while institutional and comparative studies gather momentum. Why should that be? The critical enterprise is not necessarily incompatible with the others, for the peculiar excellence of Bailyn's book lies in the fact that it embodies all three. It reveals a structure of thought; it rests on a comparative view of English and American institutions and ideas; and it is withal a committed, affirmative book which carries the reader deep into the feelings—one might say the very soul—of the American Revolution. Why do so few of today's professional historians operate with distinction in that third dimension? Why do so few probe sensitively into the values men live by and the quality of their choices?

Before trying to answer the question directly, it may be helpful to notice that certain types of historical scholarship, which are conducive to such evaluation, seem to excite less interest than they did a few years ago. A genre that has fallen in popularity is biography, and nowhere more than in biography is the historian called upon to assess character and to estimate failure and success. The great vogue for biography, which sprang up in the 1920's and 1930's first in the reading public and then among professional historians, probably began to subside in the 1950's. But it is only in the present decade that one notices a dwindling in the number of major biographical enterprises that are active, a paucity of good biographies of any sort, and a reluctance on the part of students to undertake dissertations on individuals.

A second genre, which is equally relevant to moral criticism and which may also have passed the zenith of its influence, is intellectual history. As a study of what men have believed, intellectual history has played in the twentieth century a tremendously important part in the criticism as well as the understanding of the past. Biography and intellectual history achieved academic influence and respectability between the two World Wars, biography being somewhat in the lead since it presented fewer conceptual problems. Both of them expressed an increasing dissatisfaction with the formalism and impersonality of the old institutional history. Both of them became, in effect, means of resisting the predominantly deterministic cast of American scholarship and thereby reasserting a dimension of subjectivity and freedom in human affairs.[26] An honest examination of the contemporary scene must now ask if intellectual history is beginning to be affected by the same shift of interest that has already hurt biography. Are both types of scholarship losing a former position of leadership through a swing back to institutional history and a concomitant growth of quantifiable, behavioral studies?

Only time, of course, can answer that question. But it is impossible to conceive of any general dissipation of the hard-won insight American historians have gained into the beliefs, fears, and aspirations of groups and individuals. The insights and methods of intellectual history have become an essential part of the working equipment of any historian who strives to be more than a narrow specialist. As for the specialized tasks of the intellectual historian as such, it is not impossible that they will be better managed and understood by a more discriminating and selective company of students now that intellectual history no longer seems to unlock every secret of the past. Surely the real problem is not a maldistribution of effort between fields. Is it not instead a broader inequality between the humanistic and the scientific sides of American historiography today? Biography and moral criticism may be lagging relative to institutional and comparative work because the qualitative and expressive aspect of history is cultivated in American universities less seriously than the quantitative and analytic aspect.

Here we touch on the two general predictions I made about historical theory and practice. Have historical scholars in fact in the 1960's achieved a triumphant fusion of clashing methodologies and a consequent integration in our historiography of the two cultures, the humanistic and the scientific? Have historians found a stronger, more eloquent public voice than they had a generation ago? The answer, on both counts, is most decidedly no. And our failure on the methodological and conceptual levels leads directly to the ineffectuality of our impact.

What misled me into supposing that history might be recovering the breadth of view and of relevance it had had at its best in the nineteenth century? Chiefly, I think, I was unduly encouraged by the waning of academic provincialism, especially the decline among historians of a reactionary resistance to the social sciences. Historians seemed to be losing an inferiority complex, and so they were becoming more able to learn from others—more capable of strengthening their own narrative synthesis of the human story with the wisdom of systematic disciplines. This estimate, which was true enough so far as it went, presupposed that the traditional goals and humane values of history would remain undimmed, that they would in fact be enhanced by the additional power of analysis. I failed to appreciate that mere receptiveness to new tendencies is not enough. If history is to realize its distinctive form and mission, its humanistic aspects must grow as aggressively, must be preached as ardently, must be cultivated as assiduously, as its scientific aspects. What we have at the present time in the American historical profession is an increasingly effective, well organized, laudable effort to teach young historians to think analytically and to measure precisely, *but no comparable effort* to educate their artistic and moral sensibilities. Where can a student find a graduate program that assumes as a genuine obligation a really serious study of history as a literary form? Where is there careful consideration of the problems and types of historical synthesis? Where does the study of historical methods really probe the relation between scholarship and social action in its full complexity and difficulty? Where do we turn for a research council sponsoring humanistic studies with the funds, the coordinated energy, and the dedication that have enriched the scientific dimension of history during the last forty years?

I know it is considered bad form, to say the least, to distinguish sharply between humanistic and scientific knowledge. We want no jealous sovereignties in the empire of the mind. But the fact remains that competition between different sets of aptitudes and skills in a realm as open-ended as history is unavoidable and, if properly managed, very productive. The capacity of the historian to stand between the humanities and the sciences, and to cultivate an integral view of human experience, depends upon that competition; for he must somehow accept the discipline of both science and art while resisting the limitations of each. Few historians are likely to strive for such an integral vision if their education fails to make it operational and if their contemporary culture does not inspire it.

In this connection the current trend toward quantification in history calls for a response more complex than either its partisans or its critics make. On the positive side the new quantitative methods are adding a great deal to the empirical and conceptual resources of historians. Empirically, they are opening up a level of historical reality only glimpsed by earlier scholars. The manipulation of statistical data is revealing directly the behavior of large bodies of people—their family life, social aspirations, economic condition, political choices—hitherto known only through the statements and deeds of a few leaders and observers. We can reconstitute a way of life that was never clearly understood by its participants; and we can also make reliable comparisons over long spans of time. Conceptually, this type of scholarship is encouraging a style of thought with which historians have had little familiarity. To establish conclusions by quantitative measures calls for a specification of hypotheses and an adherence to deductive procedures, which are more truly scientific than most historical thinking. Through quantification an increasing number of historians are experiencing the same delights of puzzle-solving that make up the fascination of "normal science" as Thomas Kuhn has described it.[27]

A negative judgment may also be entered against the new methods. The scientific approach, concerned as it is with general laws, breaks down the complex structures of history into simpler, more manageable, and more abstract entities. Of course there is nothing intrinsically undesirable about that; but it generates a body of theory about selected relationships at the expense of a contextual feeling—which historians ordinarily cultivate—for the many sidedness of a whole situation. In its role as a science, history surrenders one of its most distinctive functions. It does not supply a multidimensional synthesis of concrete experience; it gives no synoptic judgment of the multitudinous diversity of phenomena that belong together in the fluid continuity of occurrence. Ideally, of course, the two types of inquiry should fertilize each other. The extension of quantitative regularities should correct and enlarge the dimensions of qualitative synthesis, which in turn should pose fresh problems for statistical test. In actual practice the new scientific history induces a certain intolerance for impressionistic scholarship, with all of its imprecision and unsystematic shape.

Whether this intolerance can be offset by an equally vigorous commitment to historical synthesis may depend on the degree to which contemporary man will accept the complexity of history as meaningful and coherent. The analytical movement in history, in addition to its own positive intellectual appeal, may also have a negative function comparable to that of the analytical movement in contemporary philosophy. Do not both enterprises relieve students of the burden of a more or less comprehensive view? Do not both of them jettison a responsibility that many scholars now find too heavy to bear?

My point is that humanistic strategies make an indispensable contribution toward the coherence of history, but that coherence has become in our time much less plausible and compelling than it used to be. This is because a general framework for understanding American history has collapsed. Not only the magisterial narratives of yesteryear but all forms of general interpretation are in short supply. The proposals we have on hand, ranging all the way from Turner's frontier hypothesis to the consensus theories propounded not very long ago by Louis Hartz and Daniel Boorstin, now sell at a heavy discount. Consequently we have today no unifying theme which assigns a direction to American history and commands any wide acceptance among those who write it. Nothing in the current situation of the historian more seriously compromises his civic function and influence.

Does this mean that history will dissolve except as it becomes assimilated into the various social sciences? I do not think so. Men need a unifying vision of who they are and where they are going. That kind of vision establishes both a goal for the future and a synthesizing perspective upon the past. Without it, a fully human life is impossible.

How and where we shall find a new set of coordinates for charting directions is not at all clear. Perhaps they can no longer be located specifically in American history; it is possible that the very concept of national history is becoming outworn. To order our historical knowledge in the years ahead we may have to depend increasingly on a wider view of the nature and destiny of modern society. That *some* general scheme of historical meaning will emerge from the present confusion can scarcely be doubted, however. We may also be confident that an effective scheme will transcend the limits of a scientific hypothesis. It will partake as well of myth and ideology. It will both challenge and elude quantitative formulations, and we will then have much less need for concern about fruitful dialogue between the humanistic and the scientific aspects of historiography.

# NOTES

## CHAPTER I

1. *AHA Newsletter,* I (June, 1963), 1; address by Barnaby Keeney at the Conference on the Princeton Studies in the Humanities, Nov. 5, 1965, Nassau Inn, Princeton, N.J.

2. U.S. Congress, Senate, Committee on Labor and Public Welfare, United States Senate, *National Arts and Humanities Foundations: Hearings* [hereafter cited as *Hearings*], 89 Cong., 1 sess. (Washington, D.C., 1965), 228–30.

3. Plans for establishing a national theater, propounded before World War II by Robert Sherwood, were further developed in the late 1940's by Congressman Jacob Javits and others. Proposals for some kind of National Arts Council came before every Congress from 1955 to 1964, when a National Council on the Arts was at last created. Meanwhile, in the early 1960's, state arts councils and publicly subsidized cultural centers proliferated. (*New York Times,* Jan. 30, 1949; *Congressional Quarterly Almanac* [hereafter cited as *CQ Almanac*], XX, 88 Cong., 2 sess. [Washington, D.C., 1964], 427–29.)

4. American Council of Learned Societies, Council of Graduate Schools in the United States, United Chapters of Phi Beta Kappa, *Report of the Commission on the Humanities* (New York, 1964); see also the reports of the work of the commission in *Journal of Higher Education,* XXXVI (Jan., 1965), 5–14.

5. *New York Times,* Mar. 11, May 26, 1965. On the genesis and fate of the original proposal for an arts foundation, see Arthur M. Schlesinger, Jr., *A Thousand Days: John F. Kennedy in the White House* (Boston, 1965), 729–36, and *CQ Almanac,* 427–28.

6. Washington *Post,* Sept. 30, 1965; "Biting the Hand," *New Republic,* CLIII (Oct. 2, 1965), 8. Congressman William S. Moorhead, who introduced the bill proposed by the Commission on the Humanities in August 1964, sought an initial appropriation of only $150,000. *Journal of Higher Education,* 7–9.

7. *Hearings,* 225.

8. National Science Foundation, *Thirteenth Annual Report, 1963* (Washington, D.C., 1964), 28–29. Indeed, the NSF has continually had to vindicate its scientific neutrality to anti-intellectual congressmen.

9. Public Law 89–209 (Sept. 29, 1965), 1.

10. The controversy following the publication of Charles Percy Snow's *The Two Cultures and the Scientific Revolution* (Cambridge, England, 1959) induced the *Reader's Guide to Periodical Literature* to establish in 1961 a new subject heading, "Science and the Humanities."

11. The unity of knowledge is argued, from opposite points of view, by Robert E. Lane's *The Liberties of Wit: Humanism, Criticism and the Civic Mind* (New Haven, Conn., 1961), and Michael Polanyi, *The Logic of Personal Knowledge* (Glencoe, Ill., 1961). But my own view in what follows is more indebted to the diversities emphasized by W. T. Jones, *The Sciences and the Humanities: Conflict and Reconciliation* (Berkeley and Los Angeles, 1965), and by the stimulating symposium, *Science and Culture, A Study of Cohesive and Disjunctive Forces,* ed. Gerald Holton (Boston, 1965). For other recent discussions of the same issues, see F. S. C. Northrop, *The Logic of the Sciences and the Humanities* (New York, 1959), and Moody E. Prior, *Science and the Humanities* (Evanston, Ill., 1964).

12. Liam Hudson, *Contrary Imaginations: A Psychological Study of the English Schoolboy* (Harmondsworth, England, 1967), which is amplified in some directions by the same author's *Frames of Mind: Ability, Perception and Self-Perception in the Arts and Sciences* (London, 1968).

13. British Council, *Higher Education in the United Kingdom* (rev. ed., London, 1954), 15; Oliver C. Carmichael, *Universities, Commonwealth and American: A Comparative Study* (New York, 1959), 352.

14. United Nations Economic and Social Council, *The University Teaching of Social Sciences: Sociology, Social Psychology, and Anthropology* (Paris, 1954), 199–200.

15. *Proceedings of the British Academy,* 1903–1904, xii; Lord Robbins, *Presidential Address, 7 July 1965* (reprinted from *Proceedings of the British Academy,* LI), 5–7.

16. British Academy, *Research in the Humanities and the Social Sciences: Report of a Survey, 1958–1960* (London, 1961), 91–95; Centre National de la Recherche Scientifique, *Rapport d'Activité Octobre 1963–Octobre 1964* (Paris, 1965), 22–23.

17. For background, see Secretary of State for Education and Science, *Report of the Committee on Social Studies* (Parliamentary Papers, cmd. 2660, June, 1965); London *Times,* Aug. 6, 1965.

18. John William Adamson, *English Education, 1789–1902* (Cambridge, England, 1930), 70–95, 171–201, 236–57, 295–321, 387–446; R. C. Jebb, *Humanism in Education: The Romanes Lecture, 1899* (London, 1899).

19. Matthew Arnold, *Schools and Universities on the Continent,* in

*The Complete Prose Works of Matthew Arnold,* ed. R. H. Super (5 vols. to date, Ann Arbor, Mich., 1960–65), IV, 290–302; see also "Literature and Science," in *The Portable Matthew Arnold,* ed. Lionel Trilling (New York, 1949), 405–29.

20. Willystine Goodsell, *The Conflict of Naturalism and Humanism* (New York, 1910), 129, 161–78. The earliest examples of American usage that I have found, in an admittedly desultory search, are a defense by a professor at William and Mary College of "the Oxford order of the Humanities" and James Russell Lowell's address of 1886 at the two hundred fiftieth anniversary of Harvard College. The humanities do not figure as such in the major policy statements on higher education, such as the Yale Report of 1828. See Henry A. Wise, *Seven Decades of the Union* (Philadelphia, 1881), 314–20; *The Writings of James Russell Lowell* (10 vols., Boston, 1890), VI, 147, 160–61.

21. My discussion of the nineteenth century owes much to Laurence Veysey's impressive work, *The Emergence of the American University* (Chicago, 1965), and to the author's personal advice, though I suspect there was more blurring and accommodation between competing ideals than he allows. See also Russell Thomas, *The Search for a Common Learning: General Education, 1800–1960* (New York, 1962), 24–50.

22. W. P. Atkinson, "Liberal Education in the Nineteenth Century," *Addresses and Journal of Proceedings of the National Educational Association, 1873,* pp. 141–63; R. M. Wenley, "Transition of What?" *Educational Review,* XXXIII (May, 1907), 441–51.

For a different but related expression of American eclecticism, see James Mark Baldwin, *Darwin and the Humanities* (London, 1910), 2. Here the humanities are conceived to be continuous with the natural sciences and are said to embrace "the mental and moral sciences proper, the political and historical sciences, also, and the sciences of language and of race. . . ." While claiming to deal only with "the first of these great divisions of the humanities," Baldwin has chapters on psychology, the social sciences, ethics, logic, philosophy, and religion.

23. A. Lawrence Lowell, *At War with Academic Traditions in America* (Cambridge, Mass., 1934), 105; William Rainey Harper, *The Trend in Higher Education* (Chicago, 1905), 288; William A. Neilson, "The Inaugural Address of the President of Smith College," *School and Society,* VIII (July 20, 1918), 62–64. Lowell's address dates from 1914.

24. John Higham et al., *History* (Englewood Cliffs, N.J., 1965), 96–97, 158–70; Frank G. Hubbard, "The Undergraduate Curriculum in English Literature," *Publications of the Modern Language Association,* XXIII (No. 2, 1908), 257–64. For philosophy, see Mary Whiton Calkins's famous textbook, *The Persistent Problems of Philosophy* (rev. ed., New York, 1917).

25. It is instructive to compare Cather's elegiac portrait of the historical scholar with the devastating depiction of a similar personage in Edward Albee's *Who's Afraid of Virginia Woolf?* Cather's professor has

lost power, has almost lost the will to live, but his integrity endures: he continues to establish the moral center of his world. A generation later, in Albee's play, the custodian of the past has become empty, futile, and irrelevant.

26. K. M. Baker, "The Early History of the Term 'Social Sciences,'" *Annals of Science,* XX (1964), 211–26; Georg G. Iggers, "Further Remarks about Early Uses of the Term 'Social Science,'" *Journal of the History of Ideas,* XX (June–Sept., 1959), 433–36.

27. For the first tendency see Herbert Spencer, *The Study of Sociology* (London, 1873), Henry C. Carey, *Principles of Social Science* (3 vols., Philadelphia, 1858–59), and the work of Carey's disciple, Robert E. Thompson, *Social Science and National Economy* (Philadelphia, 1875). For the second tendency see the *Journal of Social Science* (1869–1909), Andrew Dickson White, *Instruction in Social Science* (n.p., 1891), and *The International Cyclopaedia* (15 vols., New York, 1900), XIII, 608. As recently as 1923 a standard encyclopedia defined social science as the practical branch of sociology. See *Encyclopedia Americana* (30 vols., New York, 1923), XXV, 187.

28. Edmund J. James, "The Place of the Political and Social Sciences in Modern Education," *Annals of the American Academy of Political and Social Science,* X (Nov., 1897), 380–81.

29. But around 1910 and after, an increasing consciousness of the importance and potential unity of the social sciences becomes evident in such writings as Albion W. Small, *The Meaning of Social Science* (Chicago, 1910), and A. B. Wolfe, "The Place of the Social Sciences in College Education," *Educational Review,* XXXVIII (June, 1909), 58–84.

30. John Dewey, *The Educational Situation* (Chicago, 1902), 83–98. How far Americans then were from our present classification of knowledge is indicated by the scheme adopted in 1904 by the Congress of Arts and Science at the St. Louis World's Fair. Strongly influenced by German ideas, the congress divided the "sciences of man" into three main groups: general history, including the history of law, religion, language, literature, and art; the social sciences, including anthropology, psychology, and sociology; and the "practical" studies of economics, politics, education, and religion. Jurgen Herbst, *The German Historical School in American Scholarship: A Study in the Transfer of Culture* (Ithaca, N.Y., 1965), 208.

31. Waldo G. Leland, "The Organization of the International Union of Academies and of the American Council of Learned Societies," *ACLS Bulletin* (Oct., 1920), 1–7; "The American Council of Learned Societies," *American Historical Review,* XXV (Apr., 1920), 440–47; Waldo G. Leland to Conyers Read, Jan. 9, 1933, Files of the American Historical Association, 1933–37, Manuscript Division, Library of Congress.

32. Higham et al., *History,* 104–16.

33. Frederick A. Ogg, *Research in the Humanistic and Social Sciences* (New York, 1928), 3–4.

34. Raymond B. Fosdick, *The Story of the Rockefeller Foundation* (New York, 1952), 138; Patricia Beesley, *The Revival of the Humanities in American Education* (New York, 1940); Harold B. Dunkel, *General Education in the Humanities* (Washington, D.C., 1947); Russell Thomas, *The Search for a Common Learning: General Education, 1800–1960* (New York, 1962), 64–73, 84–86.

35. *General Education in a Free Society: Report of the Harvard Committee* (Cambridge, Mass., 1945), 58–63, 67.

36. Barry Dean Karl, *Executive Reorganization and Reform in the New Deal: The Genesis of Administrative Management, 1900–1939* (Cambridge, Mass., 1963), 46. The SSRC desired the participation of the American Historical Association from the outset. After holding out for two years, the AHA came in; the financial resources the council was attracting by 1925 made further aloofness distinctly impolitic. Historians have always fared well in the distribution of individual fellowships and research grants by the SSRC; they rarely participated in its collaborative projects. The council found it difficult to relate history to the other disciplines, at least partly because of the changes those disciplines were undergoing. (See correspondence of Leland, 1924–26, in AHA Files; Roy F. Nichols, "History and the Social Science Research Council," *American Historical Review*, L (Apr., 1945), 491–99; R. D. Challener and Maurice Lee, Jr., "History and the Social Sciences: The Problem of Communications," *ibid.*, LXI (Jan., 1956), 331–38.

37. *Encyclopaedia of the Social Sciences* (15 vols., New York, 1930–35), I, xvii. On the formation of the SSRC and the development of the social sciences in the 1920's, see Fosdick, *Rockefeller Foundation*, 194–99; Herbert Heaton, *A Scholar in Action: Edwin F. Gay* (Cambridge, Mass., 1952), 206–09; Bernard Crick, *The American Science of Politics: Its Origins and Conditions* (Berkeley, Cal., 1959), 137 ff.

38. In addition to Crick's somewhat lurid account, see Wilfrid E. Rumble, Jr., "Legal Realism, Sociological Jurisprudence and Mr. Justice Holmes," *Journal of the History of Ideas*, XXVI (Oct.–Dec., 1965), 547–66; Floyd W. Matson, *The Broken Image: Man, Science, and Society* (New York, 1964), 47–65; Edward A. Shils, "The Contemplation of Society in America," in *Paths of American Thought*, ed. Arthur M. Schlesinger and Morton G. White (Boston, 1963), 392–410.

39. Robert S. Lynd, *Knowledge for What? The Place of Social Science in American Culture* (Princeton, N.J., 1939), 183–84; David Easton, "Shifting Images of Social Science and Values," *Antioch Review*, XV (Spring, 1955), 3–18.

40. But see Eric R. Wolf's perceptive account of recent changes in this respect in *Anthropology* (Englewood Cliffs, N.J., 1964).

41. Waldo G. Leland, "The American Council of Learned Societies and Its Relation to Humanistic Studies," *Proceedings of the American Philosophical Society*, LXXI (No. 4, 1932), 179–89.

42. Of course the twentieth century revolt against history has been

international, as Hayden V. White shows in "The Burden of History," *History and Theory*, V (No. 2, 1966), 113–22. But the European writers whom White quotes tell us nothing about the academic community.

43. Babbitt's program remained essentially unchanged from the publication of his first collection of essays, *Literature and the American College* (Boston, 1908). It was only in the 1920's, however, that he attracted the kind of aggressive following that could constitute a significant intellectual movement.

44. Walter Sutton, *Modern American Criticism* (Englewood Cliffs, N.J., 1963), 6–20, 175–218; Morton G. White, *Religion, Politics, and the Higher Learning: A Collection of Essays* (Cambridge, Mass., 1959), 54–55; Higham et al., *History*, 117–20, 138.

45. Waldo G. Leland, "Recent Trends in the Humanities," *Science*, LXXIX (Mar. 30, 1934), 281–82; see also Abraham Flexner, *The Burden of Humanism* (Oxford, England, 1928).

46. Fosdick, *Rockefeller Foundation*, 239–42; Beesley, *Revival of the Humanities*, vii, 3.

47. *The Meaning of the Humanities: Five Essays*, ed. Theodore M. Greene (Princeton, N.J., 1938); William A. Neilson, "The Future of the Humanities," *Harper's Magazine*, CLXXXVI (Mar., 1943), 388–91; Dorothy Hall Smith, "The Humanities Begin to Fight," *School and Society*, LVIII (Dec. 25, 1943), 481–84; C. J. Ducasse, "Are the Humanities Worth Their Keep?" *American Scholar*, VI (Oct. 1937), 460–70; Stuart G. Brown, "War and the Humanities," *Virginia Quarterly Review*, XVIII (Apr., 1942), 260–66; *A State University Surveys the Humanities*, ed. Loren MacKinney (Chapel Hill, N.C., 1945); Fred B. Millett, *The Rebirth of Liberal Education* (New York, 1945); Jacques Maritain, *Education at the Crossroads* (New Haven, Conn., 1943); David H. Stevens, *The Changing Humanities: An Appraisal of Old Values and New Uses* (New York, 1953); David Daiches, *English Literature* (Englewood Cliffs, N.J., 1965), 153–55.

48. Millett, *Rebirth,* 135.

49. Willard Thorp, "Exodus: Four Decades of American Literary Scholarship," *Modern Language Quarterly*, XXVI (Mar., 1965), 40–61. In the field of art history James Ackerman sees a lagging but necessary movement in the same direction. (James S. Ackerman and Rhys Carpenter, *Art and Archaeology* [Englewood Cliffs, N.J., 1963], 139–41, 187–95.)

50. Andrew F. West, "The Humanities after the War," *Educational Review*, LVII (Feb., 1919), 141–43; William Osler, *The Old Humanities and the New Science* (Boston, 1920), 10–11.

51. Beesley, *Revival of the Humanities*, vii; Roscoe Pound, "The Fight for Intellectual Freedom," *Vital Speeches*, V (Mar. 15, 1939), 342. How these feelings affected one field of scholarship is demonstrated in Robert Skotheim, *American Intellectual Histories and Historians* (Princeton, N.J., 1966), 244–55.

52. David Riesman, "Innovation and Reaction in Higher Education," in *Humanistic Education and Western Civilization: Essays for Robert M. Hutchins,* ed. Arthur A. Cohen (New York, 1964), 182–205.

53. Norman S. Care, "Is Philosophy Dead Too?" *New Republic,* CLIV (May 21, 1966), 23–26.

54. National Endowment for the Humanities, *Third Annual Report* (Washington, D.C., 1969), 43.

## CHAPTER 2

1. Evidence of the vogue of this distinction among professional historians is in T. C. Cochran, "A Decade of American Histories," *Pennsylvania Magazine of History and Biography,* LXXIII (1949), 154–55; W. T. Hutchinson in *American Historical Review,* LVIII (1952), 126.

2. Crane Brinton, *Ideas and Men: The Story of Western Thought* (New York, 1950), 7.

3. Merle Curti's *The Growth of American Thought* (New York, 1942) brought the distinction I am making clearly into view; see p. vi. Arthur O. Lovejoy has ably defended his own internal approach in "Reflections on the History of Ideas," *Journal of the History of Ideas,* I (1940), 3–23. I have also profited from the attack on this position in Bert J. Loewenberg, *The History of Ideas: 1935–1945; Retrospect and Prospect* (New York, 1947), 13–18.

4. S. K. Langer, *Philosophy in a New Key* (New York, 1948), 24–33.

5. Vernon L. Parrington, *Main Currents in American Thought,* 3 vols. (New York, 1927–30); Erich Fromm, *Escape from Freedom* (New York, 1941).

6. I refer to American scholarship, the divergence being much more noticeable here than in Europe, where a positivistic tradition has not had so commanding an influence over the social sciences. See E. K. Francis, "History and the Social Sciences: Some Reflections on the Reintegration of Social Science," *Review of Politics,* XIII (1951), 354–74.

7. M. G. White, *Social Thought in America: The Revolt Against Formalism* (New York, 1949).

8. Humanists, of course, vigorously disputed the claim of many social scientists to the possession of a more objective kind of knowledge. I am myself convinced that the conclusions attainable by humanistic methods are no less true than those reached by the most elaborate devices of impersonal measurement; but social scientists have been characteristically insistent on developing better (or at least more impressive) techniques of objective analysis. Humanistic scholars must employ such subjective concepts as evil, will, etc., and do not shrink from doing so.

## CHAPTER 3

1. George Bancroft, *History of the United States of America from the*

*Discovery of the Continent* (6 vols., Centenary Edition, Boston, 1876), III, 3–4. For exuberant passages of intellectual history see III, 98–104; VI, 71–75.

2. Ernst Cassirer, *The Philosophy of the Enlightenment* (Princeton, 1951), 216–25, should be qualified by the deeper analysis of Voltaire's historical work in Karl J. Weintraub, *Visions of Culture* (Chicago, 1966), 19–74.

3. Gilbert Chinard has published an appreciative essay, "Progress and Perfectibility in Samuel Miller's Intellectual History," in The Johns Hopkins University, History of Ideas Club, *Studies in Intellectual History* (Baltimore, 1953), 94–122. But I think that Chinard does not sufficiently credit the secular optimism in Miller's book, which was directed as much against conservatives who sneered at modern times as it was against utopian radicals. Miller believed that intellectual progress could not alone accomplish the progress of virtue and happiness but nevertheless tended to promote it. See I, iv–v; II, 297, 440.

4. Samuel Miller, *The Life of Samuel Miller, D.D., LL.D.* (Philadelphia, 1869), 128–33.

5. Charles F. Mullett has written on Lecky, and Sidney A. Burrell on Stephen, in *Some Modern Historians of Britain,* ed. Herman Ausubel (New York, 1951), 111–49. There is a useful chapter, "The History of Civilization," in G. P. Gooch, *History and Historians in the Nineteenth Century* (2nd ed., Boston, 1959), 523–42. See also Donald Fleming, *John William Draper and the Religion of Science* (Philadelphia, 1950). The German tradition of cultural history, the foremost exemplar of which was Jakob Burckhardt, assumed a very different character, but I have not touched upon it because it had curiously little influence in the United States until the 1930's.

6. Lecky, *History of Rationalism* (New York, 1955), I, xi, xvi; Stephen, *English Thought* (New York, 1876), I, 17–18. For their criticism of Buckle see Giles St. Aubyn, *A Victorian Eminence: The Life and Works of Henry Thomas Buckle* (London, 1958), 170, 173, 182. There is a brief discussion of the rise of the history of thought in John Theodore Merz, *A History of European Thought in the Nineteenth Century* (4 vols., Edinburgh, 1896), 1, 24–26.

7. Among American books of this sort, in addition to Draper's see: Andrew Dickson White, *The Warfare of Science* (New York, 1876); Charles Francis Adams, Jr., *Massachusetts, Its Historians and Its History* (Boston, 1893).

8. *History of Rationalism* I, xi.

9. Ibid., xi–xix. For a similar statement of objectives phrased in more theistic language by an American intellectual historian of the same era, see Octavius Brooks Frothingham quoted in Sydney E. Ahlstrom's Introduction to Frothingham's *Transcendentalism in New England: A History* (New York, 1959), xviii. Buckle had called attention to the

importance of the spirit of the age but was chiefly interested in its impact. Lecky and Stephen studied its content.

10. Nevertheless, they sometimes drew on an impressively wide range of materials. Barrett Wendell's chapter, "The American Intellect," in *The Cambridge Modern History* (New York, 1903), VII, 723–51, touched on law, philosophy, literature, art, science, and education.

11. John W. Draper, *History of the American Civil War* (3 vols., New York, 1867–70); William A. Dunning, *History of Political Theories, Ancient and Medieval* (New York, 1902), and *Reconstruction, Political and Economic, 1865–1877* (New York, 1907).

12. (New York, 1889), I, 176.

13. Published in Santayana's *Winds of Doctrine* (New York, 1912), 186–215.

14. See Raymond Williams, *Culture and Society, 1780–1950* (New York, 1958).

15. Henry Osborn Taylor, *Human Values and Verities* (Edinburgh, 1929), 55–59. Taylor had published an article on American colonial history shortly after graduating from college in 1878, but disgust at the "low and vulgar" quality of American life soon sent him abroad to study Roman law and Old World culture.

16. *Literary History of the American Revolution*, I, vii; Jessica Tyler Austen, ed., *Moses Coit Tyler, 1835–1900: Selections from His Letters and Diaries* (New York, 1911), 43. See also Howard Mumford Jones and Thomas Edgar Casady, *The Life of Moses Coit Tyler* (Ann Arbor, Mich., 1933).

17. *History of American Literature*, II, 24.

18. William Peterfield Trent, "Moses Coit Tyler," *Forum*, XXXI (Aug., 1901), 756.

19. Robert Allen Skotheim, *American Intellectual Histories and Historians* (Princeton, 1966), 32–61.

20. Charles H. McIlwain, *The High Court of Parliament and Its Supremacy* (New Haven, 1910); Edwin S. Corwin, *The Doctrine of Judicial Review* (Princeton, 1914), "The 'Higher Law' Background of American Constitutional Law," *Harvard Law Review*, XLII (1928–29), 149–85, 365–409, and *American Constitutional History*, ed. by Alpheus T. Mason and Gerald Garvey (New York, 1964); Andrew C. McLaughlin, "Social Compact and Constitutional Construction," *American Historical Review*, V (Apr., 1900), 467–90, and *The Foundations of American Constitutionalism* (New York, 1932). See also Herbert L. Osgood, "The Political Ideas of the Puritans," *Political Science Quarterly*, VI (1891), 1–28, 201–31.

21. Skotheim, *American Intellectual Histories*, 73–74; James Harvey Robinson, *The New History: Essays Illustrating the Modern Historical Outlook* (New York, 1912).

22. Luther V. Hendricks, *James Harvey Robinson: Teacher of His-*

*tory* (New York, 1946), 15, 103–04; Arthur M. Schlesinger, *In Retrospect: The History of a Historian* (New York, 1963), 34–35.

23. Charles A. Beard, *An Economic Interpretation of the Constitution of the United States* (New York, 1913), and *Economic Origins of Jeffersonian Democracy* (New York, 1915).

24. *Letters and Leadership* (New York, 1918), ch. III, reprinted in Van Wyck Brooks, *America's Coming-of-Age* (Garden City, N.Y., 1958), 103.

25. Warren I. Susman, "The Useless Past: American Intellectuals and the Frontier Thesis: 1910–1930," *Bucknell Review*, XI (March, 1963), 1–20; Joseph Wood Krutch, "The Usable Past," *Nation*, cxxxviii (Feb. 14, 1934), 191.

26. P. 279. As Burleigh Taylor Wilkins has pointed out, Becker anticipated here the argument of his most important book, *The Heavenly City of the Eighteenth Century Philosophers* (New Haven, 1932). See Wilkins's *Carl Becker: A Biographical Study in American Intellectual History* (Cambridge, Mass., 1961), 123.

27. Becker, *Heavenly City,* 5.

28. A competent but unexciting beginning was made on the American side by I. Woodbridge Riley in *American Philosophy: The Early Schools* (New York, 1907) and *American Thought from Puritanism to Pragmatism and Beyond* (New York, 1923). For an appraisal of Riley's work see Vincent Buranelli, "Colonial Philosophy," *William and Mary Quarterly*, XVI (July, 1959), 345–52.

29. James L. Colwell, "The Populist Image of Vernon Louis Parrington," *Mississippi Valley Historical Review*, XLIX (June, 1962), 57–58, 63–66.

30. *Main Currents in American Thought* (3 vols., New York, 1927–30), III, 402. The personal overtones of this whole chapter are revealing. I have profited from several acute appraisals of Parrington's work, though I have not always been able to follow their conclusions. See Merrill D. Peterson, "Parrington and American Liberalism," *Virginia Quarterly Review*, XXX (Winter, 1954), 35–49; Lionel Trilling, "Reality in America," in *The Liberal Imagination: Essays on Literature and Society* (Garden City, N.Y., 1953), 3–21; Skotheim, *American Intellectual Histories*, 124–48; and especially Richard Hofstadter, *The Progressive Historians: Turner, Beard, Parrington* (New York, 1968), 349–434.

31. Charles A. and Mary R. Beard, *The Rise of American Civilization* (one vol. ed., New York, 1930), vii, xi, xiv–xv. For a detailed account of the changes in Beard's outlook during the 1920's see Bernard C. Borning, *The Political and Social Thought of Charles A. Beard* (Seattle, 1962), 64–135.

32. Charles A. and Mary R. Beard, *The American Spirit: A Study of the Idea of Civilization in the United States* (New York, 1942). See also

David W. Marcell, "Charles Beard: Civilization and the Revolt Against Empiricism," *American Quarterly,* XXI (Spring, 1969), 65–86.

33. "An Editor's Second Thoughts," in *Approaches to American Social History,* ed. by William E. Lingelbach (New York, 1937), 84; Schlesinger, *In Retrospect,* 68, 77.

34. R. Richard Wohl, "Intellectual History: An Historian's View," *Historian,* XVI (1953), 62–77. Another characteristic statement is Dixon Wecter's "Ideas as Master Switches," *Saturday Review of Literature,* XXXII (Aug. 6, 1949), 64–65. Notice that Wecter's metaphor clearly assigns an instrumental role to ideas: as master switches, they complete an electrical circuit, but the source of energy is presumably elsewhere.

35. *Social Darwinism in American Thought* (Philadelphia, 1944), 176.

36. This shift may be observed, for example, in the concluding chapter of Henry F. May's *Protestant Churches and Industrial America* (New York, 1949), in the introduction to Richard Hofstadter's *The American Political Tradition and the Men Who Made It* (New York, 1948), and in the pervasive flavor of Henry Steele Commager's *The American Mind: An Interpretation of American Thought and Character Since the 1880's* (New Haven, 1950). An early and explicit example of the same shift, outside the historical profession, may be seen in H. Richard Niebuhr's *The Kingdom of God in America* (New York, 1937). In that book the author confessed that the sociological approach he had adopted in *The Social Sources of Denominationalism* (New York, 1929) failed to explain either the underlying unity or the distinctive force of American Christianity.

37. Arthur O. Lovejoy, "Reflections on the History of Ideas," *Journal of the History of Ideas,* I (Jan., 1940), 21. There are acute critiques of Lovejoy's distinctive method in: R. W. B. Lewis, "Spectroscope for Ideas," *Kenyon Review,* XVI (Spring, 1954), 313–22; Maurice Mandelbaum, "The History of Ideas, Intellectual History, and the History of Philosophy," *History and Theory,* Beiheft 5 (1965), 33–42; and Louis O. Mink, "Change and Causality in the History of Ideas," *Eighteenth Century Studies,* II (Fall, 1968), 7–25.

I do not mean to suggest that Lovejoy was primarily motivated by opposition to the New Historians. His constructive purpose rivalled but in one way paralleled theirs. Both aimed at breaching artificial divisions between academic departments. Both promoted interdisciplinary collaboration: in Lovejoy's case, among the humanities; between history and the social sciences in the case of Robinson and his followers.

38. Review of *Encyclopaedia of the Social Sciences* in *American Historical Review,* XL (Jan., 1935), 306–07; review of Stuart Rice's *Methods in Social Science,* quoted in Skotheim, *American Intellectual Histories,* 216.

39. Others were: *The Puritan Pronaos: Studies in the Intellectual Life of New England in the Seventeenth Century* (New York, 1936); *The Founding of Harvard College* (Cambridge, Mass., 1935); *Harvard College in the Seventeenth Century* (2 vols., Cambridge, Mass., 1936).

40. *Orthodoxy in Massachusetts, 1630–1650* (Cambridge, Mass., 1933), xi.

41. Gabriel, *The Course of American Democratic Thought* (2nd ed., New York, 1956), 88–89; Morison, *Puritan Pronaos,* 10–11. For an example of the contrast between adaptation and intervention, compare the first section of Gabriel's book with the first section of Curti's *Growth of American Thought.* One was entitled "The Doctrines of the American Democratic Faith Examined and Set Against the Social and Intellectual Background," the other "Adaptation of the European Heritage."

42. I am indebted here to David A. Hollinger's perceptive article, "Perry Miller and Philosophical History," *History and Theory,* VII (1968), 189–202.

43. Gene Wise, "Implicit Irony in Perry Miller's *New England Mind,*" *Journal of the History of Ideas,* XXIX (Oct.-Dec., 1968), 579–600. See also Richard Reinitz, "Perry Miller and Recent American Historiography," *Bulletin of the British Association for American Studies* (June, 1964), 27–35, and essays by Donald Fleming, Alan Heimert, and Edmund S. Morgan, "Perry Miller and the American Mind," *The Harvard Review,* II (Winter–Spring, 1964).

44. See especially "From Edwards to Emerson," in *Errand into the Wilderness* (Cambridge, Mass., 1956), 184–203; "From the Covenant to the Revival," in *Nature's Nation* (Cambridge, Mass., 1967), 90–120; and the primary emphasis given to revivalism in *The Life of the Mind in America* (New York, 1965).

45. An early report, written from a historian's point of view, is in Richard H. Shryock, "The Nature and Implications of Programs in American Civilization," *American Heritage,* III (April, 1949), 36–43.

46. Henry Nash Smith has been very much interested in both questions, which is one reason why *Virgin Land* was an unusually suggestive book. On the tension between Smith's interest in myth and his interest in environment, see Barry Marks, "The Concept of Myth in *Virgin Land,*" *American Quarterly,* V (1953), 71–76.

47. Thomas C. Cochran, "A Decade of American Histories," *Pennsylvania Magazine of History of Biography,* LXXIII (April, 1949), 152; John D. Hicks to Guy Stanton Ford, February 20, 1947, "Appointments —Openings 1947," Archives of the American Historical Association (Division of Manuscripts, Library of Congress).

48. Stow Persons, *American Minds: A History of Ideas* (New York, 1958); Henry F. May, *The End of American Innocence: A Study of the First Years of Our Own Time, 1912–1917* (New York, 1959).

49. For a further account, see below, pp. 143–46.

50. Skotheim, *American Intellectual Histories,* 286.

51. One of the most remarkable historians who came to the fore in the 1950's, Daniel J. Boorstin, developed a kind of intellectual or cultural history that eliminated rational ideological systems entirely. Thought and behavior blended indistinguishably in a history premised on the "amorphousness" of America, the "peculiar incoherence" of any period, and the overall "formlessness of American thought." See especially *The Americans: The National Experience* (New York, 1965), and Boorstin's statement of method in *America and the Image of Europe: Reflections on American Thought* (New York, 1960), 43–78.

52. Warren I. Susman, "History and the American Intellectual: Uses of a Usable Past," *American Quarterly*, XVI (Summer, 1964), 243–63.

53. For a partial exception see Staughton Lynd, *Intellectual Origins of American Radicalism* (New York, 1968). But Lynd's interest in the genealogy of contemporary radicalism runs counter to the emotional disengagement from the past, which seems to be more characteristic of dissent today.

54. In addition to Weintraub's *Visions of Culture*, I have found the following articles helpful: Felix Gilbert, "Cultural History and Its Problems," in XI Congrès International des Sciences Historiques, *Rapports* (1960), I, 40–58; David Brion Davis, "Some Recent Directions in American Cultural History," *American Historical Review*, LXXIII (Feb., 1968), 696–707; John William Ward, "History and the Concept of Culture," in *Red, White, and Blue: Men, Books, and Ideas in American Culture* (New York, 1969), 3–17.

CHAPTER 4

1. Henry Steele Commager, *The American Mind: An Interpretation of American Thought and Character Since the 1880's* (New Haven, 1950), ch. 2.

2. Marcus Cunliffe, "American Watersheds," *American Quarterly*, XIII (Winter, 1961), 480–94.

3. Gerhard Masur, *Prophets of Yesterday: Studies in European Culture, 1890–1914* (New York, 1961); H. Stuart Hughes, *Consciousness and Society: The Reorientation of European Social Thought, 1890–1930* (New York, 1958); Morse Peckham, *Beyond the Tragic Vision: The Quest for Identity in the Nineteenth Century* (New York, 1962); Roger Shattuck, *The Banquet Years: The Arts in France, 1885–1918* (Garden City, 1961); Carl E. Schorske, "Politics and the Psyche in *fin de siècle* Vienna: Schnitzler and Hofmannsthal," *American Historical Review*, LXVI (July, 1961), 930–46; and Eugen Weber, "The Secret World of Jean Barois: Notes on the Portrait of an Age," in *The Origins of Modern Consciousness*, ed. John Weiss (Detroit, 1965), 79–109.

4. Philippe Ariès, *Centuries of Childhood: A Social History of Family Life* (New York, 1965), 29–30; Ernest Earnest, *Academic Procession:*

*An Informal History of the American College, 1636 to 1953* (Indianapolis, 1953), 204–36.

5. Robert H. Boyle, *Sport—Mirror of American Life* (Boston, 1963), 241–71.

6. Allan Houston Macdonald, *Richard Hovey, Man & Craftsman* (Durham, N.C., 1957), 128–29.

7. Frederick Rudolph, *The American College and University: A History* (New York, 1962), 373–93; Earnest, *Academic Procession*, 220–29; Foster Rhea Dulles, *America Learns to Play* (Gloucester, Mass., 1959), 264; John Allen Krout, *Annals of American Sport* (New Haven, 1929), 225.

8. Theodore Roosevelt, *The Strenuous Life: Essays and Addresses* (New York, 1900), 8, 20–21.

9. *The Selected Writings of John Jay Chapman,* ed. Jacques Barzun (New York, 1957), 248–50; Henry James, *The Ambassadors* (New York, 1930), 149. On James's significance in this respect, see Philip Rahv, *Image and Idea: Twenty Essays on Literary Themes* (Norfolk, Conn., 1957), 7–25.

10. *A Dictionary of Americanisms on Historical Principles,* ed. Mitford M. Mathews (Chicago, 1951). On "stuffed shirt" see also Thomas Beer, *Hanna, Crane, and The Mauve Decade* (New York, 1941), 97.

11. "Recording Time of Employees," *Scientific American,* LXIX (Aug. 12, 1893), 101.

12. Frank Luther Mott, *A History of American Magazines, 1885–1905* (Cambridge, Mass., 1957), 369–70, 377–78; Frederick W. Cozens and Florence S. Stumpf, *Sports in American Life* (Chicago, 1953), 155; Harold Seymour, *Baseball: The Early Years* (New York, 1960), 345–58.

13. Dulles, *America Learns to Play,* 226–27; Krout, *Annals,* 227–31.

14. Mott, *American Magazines,* 316–17; Robert Lewis Taylor, "Physical Culture," *New Yorker,* XXVI (Oct. 21, 1950), 47–50.

15. Roderick Nash, *Wilderness and the American Mind* (New Haven, 1967), 108–60; Lawrence A. Cremin, *The Transformation of the School: Progressivism in American Education, 1876–1957* (New York, 1961), 77; Margaret H. Underwood, *Bibliography of North American Minor Natural History Serials in the University of Michigan Libraries* (Ann Arbor, Mich., 1954). For general background see Hans Huth, *Nature and the American: Three Centuries of Changing Attitudes* (Berkeley, Cal., 1957), which reminds us that urban interest in the out-of-doors grew steadily during the preceding decades, though it increased most sharply after 1890.

16. Francis W. Halsey, "The Rise of the Nature Writers," *Review of Reviews,* XXVI (November, 1902), 567–71.

17. *Birds,* II (December, 1897), back cover; *Bird Lore,* I (1899), 28.

18. James D. Hart, *The Popular Book: A History of America's Literary Taste* (New York, 1950), 214–15; Grant C. Knight, *The Critical Period in American Literature* (Chapel Hill, N.C., 1951), 121.

19. Macdonald, *Hovey,* 141–50.

20. David Ewen, *Panorama of American Popular Music* (Englewood Cliffs, N.J., 1957), 100–05, 142; *One Hundred Years of Music in America,* ed. Paul Henry Lang (New York, 1961), 143–47; Gilbert Chase, *America's Music From the Pilgrims to the Present* (New York, 1955), 433–45. See also the detailed account by Rudi Blesh and Harriet Janis, *They All Played Ragtime: The True Story of an American Music* (New York, 1959).

21. Bernarr Macfadden, *The Power and Beauty of Superb Womanhood* (New York, 1901), 23; William Dean Howells, *Suburban Sketches* (Boston, 1872), 96; James Fullarton Muirhead, *The Land of Contrasts* (London, 1898), 127.

22. Quoted from *Munsey's Magazine,* 1896, in Mott, *American Magazines,* 370–71.

23. Eleanor Flexner, *Century of Struggle: The Woman's Rights Movement in the United States* (Cambridge, Mass., 1959), 222–25.

24. James C. Malin, *Confounded Rot about Napoleon: Reflections upon Science and Technology, Nationalism, World Depression of the Eighteen-Nineties, and Afterwards* (Lawrence, Kan., 1961), 90, 185–97.

25. Cozens and Stumpf, *Sports,* 112–14. On cheer leaders see Muirhead, *Land of Contrasts,* 114; on jingoism, Richard Hofstadter, "Manifest Destiny and the Philippines," in *America in Crisis,* ed. Daniel Aaron (New York, 1952), 173–200.

26. Isaac Goldberg, *Tin Pan Alley* (New York, 1930), 166; Krout, *Annals,* 227; Theodore Roosevelt, "Value of an Athletic Training," *Harper's Weekly,* XXXVII (Dec. 23, 1893), 1236.

27. Halsey, "Rise of the Nature Writers," *Review of Reviews,* XXVI, 571; Masur, *Prophets of Yesterday,* 356–59. The appeal of Haggard and Kipling in America is indicated in Hart, *Popular Book,* 309–10.

28. Frances Elizabeth McFall ("Sarah Grand"), *The Heavenly Twins* (New York, 1893), 193; Frank Luther Mott, *Golden Multitudes: The Story of Best Sellers in the United States* (New York, 1947), 181–82. For a comparative study of the "New Morality" in England and in America see William L. O'Neill, *Divorce in the Progressive Era* (New Haven, 1967), 142–55.

29. Muirhead, *Land of Contrasts,* 106 ff.: *Sports & Athletics in 1908* (London, 1908), 13.

30. Paul de Rousiers, *American Life* (Paris, 1892), 324–33; Nat Fleischer, *The Heavyweight Championship* (New York, 1949), xiii.

31. Holbrook Jackson, *The Eighteen Nineties* (Harmondsworth, England, 1939), 28.

32. Harry Thurston Peck, "Migration of Popular Songs," *Bookman,* II (Sept., 1895), 101; Chase, *America's Music,* 438.

33. Benedetto Croce, *History of Europe in the Nineteenth Century* (New York, 1933), 343. Croce gives a caustic appraisal of the new

activism, which he views as a "perversion of the love of liberty" and holds responsible for the failure to avert a world war in 1914.

34. Duffield Osborne, "A Defense of Pugilism," *North American Review,* CXLVI (Apr., 1888), 435; D. A. Sargent et al., *Athletic Sports* (New York, 1897), 4.

35. Walter LaFeber, *The New Empire: An Interpretation of American Expansion, 1860–1898* (Ithaca, N.Y., 1963), 63–101; Aileen S. Kraditor, *The Ideas of the Woman Suffrage Movement, 1890–1920* (New York, 1965), 97–101. There is an excellent discussion of this primitivistic theme in some of the leading novelists in Larzer Ziff, *The American 1890s: Life and Times of a Lost Generation* (New York, 1966), 173–228, 250–66.

36. Gertrude Atherton, "Why Is American Literature Bourgeois?" *North American Review,* CLXXVIII (May, 1904), 778, emphasis added.

37. Boyle, *Sport,* 6–19; Dulles, *America Learns to Play,* 171; "Boxing," *Appleton's Annual Cyclopedia,* 1888, 98–99; Duncan Edwards, "Life at the Athletic Clubs," *Scribner's Magazine,* XVIII (July, 1895), 4–23.

38. Lang, *One Hundred Years,* 147; Blesh and Janis, *They All Played Ragtime,* 152–53; James Weldon Johnson, *Black Manhattan* (New York, 1930), 105.

39. Richard Hofstadter, *The Paranoid Style in American Politics and Other Essays* (New York, 1967), 145–87; John P. Mallan, "The Warrior Critique of the Business Civilization," *American Quarterly,* VIII (Fall, 1956), 218–30; Frederick Merk, *Manifest Destiny and Mission in American History: A Reinterpretation* (New York, 1963), 143–53.

40. Robert H. Wiebe, *The Search for Order, 1877–1920* (New York, 1967).

41. Maurice F. Brown, "Santayana's American Roots," *New England Quarterly,* XXXIII (June, 1960), 147–63; Eric McKitrick, "Edgar Saltus of the Obsolete," *American Quarterly,* III (Spring, 1951), 22–35; Max I. Baym, *The French Education of Henry Adams* (New York, 1951), 67.

42. Harold Frederic, *The Damnation of Theron Ware* (New York, 1896), 484.

43. Roger B. Salomon, *Twain and the Image of History* (New Haven, 1961), 199.

44. William Graham Sumner, *Social Darwinism: Selected Essays,* ed. Stow Persons (New York, 1963), 179–80; Rollo Ogden, *Life and Letters of Edwin Lawrence Godkin,* 2 vols. (New York, 1907), II, 186–87, 199, 202.

45. Brooks Adams, *The Law of Civilization and Decay* (New York, 1895); Henry Adams, *The Degradation of the Democratic Dogma* (New York, 1920).

46. Woodrow Wilson, *Congressional Government* (Boston, 1885), 5; Barrett Wendell, *A Literary History of America* (New York, 1900), 518.

47. Richard Burton, "Degenerates and Geniuses," *The Critic,* XXV

(Aug. 11, 1894), 85–86. For a general review of this intensely animated discussion see Milton Painter Foster, "The Reception of Max Nordau's *Degeneration* in England and America," University Microfilms, No. 1807 (Ann Arbor, Mich., 1954).

48. Quoted in George Mowry, *The Era of Theodore Roosevelt, 1900–1912* (New York, 1958), 88. See also Donald Pizer, "Romantic Individualism in Garland, Norris and Crane," *American Quarterly,* X (Winter, 1958), 463–75, and Kenneth S. Lynn, *The Dream of Success: A Study of the Modern American Imagination* (Boston, 1955).

49. Van Wyck Brooks, *The Confident Years, 1885–1915* (New York, 1952), 218.

50. Arthur Beringause, *Brooks Adams, A Biography* (New York, 1955), 167–71, 186.

51. William E. Leuchtenburg, "Progressivism and Imperialism: The Progressive Movement and American Foreign Policy, 1898–1916," *Mississippi Valley Historical Review,* XXXIX (Dec., 1952), 483–504; John Higham, *Strangers in the Land: Patterns of American Nativism 1860–1925* (New Brunswick, 1955), 106–18, 144–45.

52. My indebtedness in the following pages to Morton G. White's *Social Thought in America: The Revolt Against Formalism* (New York, 1949) and to Henry F. May's *The End of American Innocence: The First Years of Our Own Time, 1912–1917* (New York, 1959) should be readily apparent, although they deal with other people and with a later period. I think the 1890's were more critically important than either book suggests.

53. On Turner's intellectual development see Fulmer Mood, "The Development of Turner as a Historial Thinker," Colonial Society of Massachusetts *Transactions,* XXXIV (1939), 283–352, and Lee Benson, *Turner and Beard: American Historical Writing Reconsidered* (Glencoe, Ill., 1960), 21–34.

54. Ralph Barton Perry, *The Thought and Character of William James,* 2 vols. (Boston, 1935), II, 251, 312.

55. "The Reminiscences of Guy Stanton Ford" (Oral History Research Office, Columbia University, 1956), 77–85; Ray Allen Billington, "Why Some Historians Rarely Write History: A Case Study of Frederick Jackson Turner," *Mississippi Valley Historical Review,* L (June, 1963), 3–27.

56. Frank Lloyd Wright, *An Autobiography* (New York, 1943). On Wright's development and qualities as an architect I am especially indebted to Vincent Scully, Jr., *Frank Lloyd Wright* (New York, 1960).

57. Perry, *James,* II, 700.

58. See especially his *Rise of the New West, 1819–1829* (New York, 1906).

59. Edward Bok, *The Americanization of Edward Bok* (New York, 1922), 238–45, 251–58.

60. Wright, *Autobiography,* 71. Cf. James's remark: "Your last two

letters have breathed a . . . *Lebenslust,* which . . . nothing but mother earth can give." Perry, *James,* I, 414.

61. Quoted in Scully, *Wright,* 18; Frederick Jackson Turner, *The Frontier in American History* (New York, 1920).

62. William James, *The Will to Believe* (New York, 1931), 39–62, and *The Varieties of Religious Experience* (Modern Library, n.d.). These books were first published in 1896 and 1902 respectively.

63. "Whitman and the Influence of Space on American Literature," Newberry Library *Bulletin,* V (Dec., 1961), 299–314.

64. James, *Varieties,* 84. In print, Turner quoted Whitman only once; he turned more readily to Kipling. *Frontier,* 262, 270, 336.

65. John Burroughs, *Whitman: A Study* (New York, 1896), 223. See also Burrough's own response to Whitman (p. 103): "He kindles in me the delight I have in space, freedom, power. . . ." On Whitman's reputation in the 1890's see Charles B. Willard, *Whitman's American Fame* (Providence, 1950), 28–29, 216.

66. Perry, *James,* II, 258; Wright, *Autobiography,* 126–28.

67. In addition to the sources cited in Note 3 above, see Arthur Symons, *The Symbolist Movement in Literature* (London, 1899). I think it is pertinent that this kind of book about dramatic new trends in contemporary American culture was not written until the second decade of the twentieth century.

68. Hamilton Wright Mabie, *Essays on Nature and Culture* (New York, 1896), 231–32, 235–36, 241.

## CHAPTER 5

1. Jarvis M. Morse, *American Beginnings: Highlights and Sidelights of the Birth of the New World* (Washington, D.C., 1952), 39. See also Richard S. Dunn, "Seventeenth-Century English Historians of America," in *Seventeenth-Century America,* ed. James Morton Smith (Chapel Hill, N.C., 1959), 195–225.

2. Quoted in Kenneth B. Murdock, *Literature and Theology in Colonial New England* (Cambridge, Mass., 1949), 92. This chapter is one of the best appraisals of the Puritan historians, but it should be supplemented by Peter Gay's striking reassessment, *A Loss of Mastery: Puritan Historians in Colonial America* (Berkeley, Cal., 1967).

3. Quoted in Herbert Heaton, *A Scholar in Action: Edwin F. Gay* (Cambridge, Mass., 1952), 16.

4. This is one of the valuable insights in J. Franklin Jameson's almost forgotten little book, *The History of Historical Writing in America* (Boston, 1891).

5. Harvey Wish, *The American Historian: A Social-Intellectual History of the Writing of the American Past* (New York, 1960), 31–57. Additional light on the motivation of the patrician historians is shed in

George H. Callcott, "Historians in Early Nineteenth-Century America," *New England Quarterly,* XXXII (Dec., 1959), 496–520.

6. *The History of the Colony and Province of Massachusetts-Bay,* ed. Lawrence Shaw Mayo (3 vols., Cambridge, Mass., 1936), II, 217–18. On another noteworthy historian of the American Revolution, see Page Smith, "David Ramsay and the Causes of the American Revolution," *William and Mary Quarterly,* XVII (Jan., 1960), 51–77.

7. The popular success of history is amply demonstrated in William Charvat, *Literary Publishing in America, 1790–1850* (Philadelphia, 1959), 74–77. For an excellent study of the principal romantic historians, see David Levin, *History as Romantic Art: Bancroft, Prescott, Motley and Parkman* (Stanford, Cal., 1959).

8. *History of the United States* (6 vols., Boston, 1849–52), I, vii. Although Hildreth was unique among the major writers, a number of minor scholars with a similarly realistic, critical outlook appeared in the 1850's. See David D. Van Tassel, *Recording America's Past, An Interpretation of the Development of Historical Studies in America, 1607–1884* (Chicago, 1960), 121–34.

9. Russel B. Nye, *George Bancroft, Brahmin Rebel* (New York, 1944). There is a different interpretation of Bancroft in David W. Noble, *Historians Against History: The Frontier Thesis and the National Covenant in American Historical Writing Since 1830* (Minneapolis, 1967).

10. Otis A. Pease, *Parkman's History: The Historian as Literary Artist* (New Haven, 1953). See also Mason Wade, *Francis Parkman, Heroic Historian* (New York, 1942), and William R. Taylor, "A Journey into the Human Mind: Motivation in Francis Parkman's *La Salle,*" *William and Mary Quarterly,* XIX (Apr., 1962), 220–37.

11. Michael Kraus, *The Writing of American History* (Norman, Okla., 1953).

12. *Letters of Henry Adams, 1858–1891,* ed. Worthington C. Ford (Boston, 1930), 357. See also William H. Jordy, *Henry Adams: Scientific Historian* (New Haven, 1952).

13. Charlotte Watkins Smith, *Carl Becker, On History and the Climate of Opinion* (Ithaca, N.Y., 1956), 15. The professionalization of history is treated at greater length in my book, *History (Humanistic Scholarship in America: The Princeton Studies,* Englewood Cliffs, N.J., 1965).

CHAPTER 6

1. Frederick Jackson Turner, *The Frontier in American History* (New York, 1920), 216.

2. H. C. Allen, "F. J. Turner and the Frontier in American History," in *British Essays in American History,* ed. H. C. Allen and C. P. Hill (New York, 1957), 145–66; Jean-Louis Rieupeyrout, *Histoire du Far*

*West* (Paris, 1967). See also the enthusiastic review of the latter by Claude Michel Cluny in *La Quinzaine littéraire,* July 15–31, 1967, 27.

3. Edwin Lawrence Godkin, *Problems of Modern Democracy: Political and Economic Essays* (New York, 1896), 49–50.

4. Henry Nash Smith, *Virgin Land: The American West as Symbol and Myth* (New York, 1957), 291–305. See also the related criticisms by George Wilson Pierson, Benjamin F. Wright, Jr., and Carlton J. H. Hayes, which have been collected in *The Turner Thesis Concerning the Role of the Frontier in American History,* ed. George Rogers Taylor (rev. ed., Boston, 1956). In an especially sweeping attack David Noble has exhibited Turner as the central figure in a long tradition of thought that associated America with nature rather than civilization. See *Historians Against History: The Frontier Thesis and the National Covenant in American Historical Writing Since 1830* (Minneapolis, 1965).

5. See Turner's *Rise of the New West, 1819–1829* (New York, 1906) and *The Significance of Sections in American History* (New York, 1932). A particularly informative and interesting book about Turner, containing the most useful bibliography available, is *The Historical World of Frederick Jackson Turner, with Selections from His Correspondence,* ed. Wilbur R. Jacobs (New Haven, 1968). See also Jacobs' excellent introduction to a companion volume, *Frederick Jackson Turner's Legacy: Unpublished Writings in American History* (San Marino, Cal., 1965).

6. "The 'Newness' of the New Nation," in *The Comparative Approach to American History,* ed. C. Vann Woodward (New York, 1968), 62–74. Hofstadter has since published a perceptive study of Turner and his critics in *The Progressive Historians: Turner, Beard, Parrington* (New York, 1968).

7. For all of the discussion of Turner's ideas, very few scholars have tried to test them by comparing communities in different sections and at different stages of social development. One exception is Merle Curti's comparison of the property structure of two rural areas in *The Making of an American Community* (Stanford, Cal., 1959), 77–80; another is Stanley Elkins' and Eric McKitrick's venturesome essay, "A Meaning for Turner's Frontier," *Political Science Quarterly,* LXIX (1954), 321–53, 565–602. One aspect of the Elkins-McKitrick formulation has been criticized in Robert R. Dykstra, *The Cattle Towns* (New York, 1968), 371–78.

8. On television see A.P. dispatch in Ann Arbor *News,* Aug. 3, 1969, p. 36. On the western film, see Charlton Ogburn, Jr., "How the West Was Lost—And Why," *New Republic,* CLIV (June 25, 1966), 34–36; J. D. Weaver, "Destry Rides Again, and Again, and Again," *Holiday,* XXXIV (Aug., 1963), 77–80.

9. *Exploration and Empire: The Explorer and the Scientist in the Winning of the American West* (New York, 1966).

10. *America's Western Frontiers: The Exploration and Settlement of the Trans-Mississippi West* (New York, 1967).

## CHAPTER 8

1. Samuel Eliot Morison, *The Puritan Pronaos: Studies in the Intellectual Life of New England in the Seventeenth Century* (New York, 1936); Walter Prescott Webb, *The Great Plains* (Boston, 1931); Carl Wittke, *We Who Built America: The Saga of the Immigrant* (New York, 1939); Ulrich B. Phillips, *Life and Labor in the Old South* (Boston, 1929); E. Merton Coulter, *The South During Reconstruction, 1865–1877* (Baton Rouge, La., 1947). Students of labor history seem also increasingly irenic; even business history may be losing an apologetic tone. The one significant exception to all of this is the new temper of Black history.

2. Avery Craven, *The Repressible Conflict, 1830–1861* (Baton Rouge, La., 1939); Samuel Flagg Bemis, *A Diplomatic History of the United States* (New York, 1950), 463–75; Thomas A. Bailey, *Woodrow Wilson and the Great Betrayal* (New York, 1945).

3. Edward P. Cheyney, *Law in History and Other Essays* (New York, 1927), 22–24; Dixon Ryan Fox, "A Synthetic Principle in American Social History," *American Historical Review,* XXXV (Jan., 1930), 256–66.

4. Frederick Paxson, *When the West Is Gone* (Boston, 1930).

5. The economic interpretation of history, Charles A. Beard wrote in 1913, "rests upon the concept that social progress in general is the result of contending interests in society—some favorable, others opposed to change." (*An Economic Interpretation of the Constitution* [rev. ed., New York, 1935], 19.)

6. Arthur Schlesinger, Sr., "Tides of American Politics," *Yale Review,* XXIX (Dec., 1939), 220.

7. George F. Kennan, *American Diplomacy 1900–1950* (Chicago, 1951).

8. The gradual revision, since World War II, of Avery Craven's revisionism has often been remarked upon. See T. N. Bonner, "Civil War Historians and the Needless War Doctrine," *Journal of the History of Ideas,* XVII (Apr., 1956), 193–216.

9. Ralph Gabriel's *The Course of American Democratic Thought: An Intellectual History Since 1815* (New York, 1940) anticipated a point of view that has become much more common since World War II in books such as Clinton Rossiter's *Seedtime of the Republic: The Origin of the American Tradition of Political Liberty* (New York, 1953), Louis Hartz's *The Liberal Tradition in America: An Interpretation of American Political Thought Since the Revolution* (New York, 1955), Robert

E. Brown's *Middle-Class Democracy and the Revolution in Massachu-setts 1691–1780* (Ithaca, N.Y., 1955), and Edmund S. and Helen M. Morgan's *The Stamp Act Crisis: Prologue to Revolution* (Chapel Hill, N.C., 1953). Perhaps the most provocative analysis of the "togetherness" of American society and the continuity of American history is Daniel J. Boorstin's *The Americans: The Colonial Experience* (New York, 1958). See also David Potter's interpretation of the unifying influence of eco-nomic abundance in American history, *People of Plenty: Economic Abundance and the American Character* (Chicago, 1954). I have criti-cized this trend at greater length in "The Cult of the 'American Con-sensus': Homogenizing Our History," *Commentary*, XXVII (Feb., 1959), 93–100, an article from which some of the remarks in the next few paragraphs are drawn.

10. Allan Simpson, "How Democratic Was Roger Williams?" *Wil-liam and Mary Quarterly*, XIII (Jan., 1956), 53–67; Wilcomb E. Wash-burn, *The Governor and the Rebel: A History of Bacon's Rebellion in Virginia* (Chapel Hill, N.C., 1957); Bray Hammond, *Banks and Politics in America from the Revolution to the Civil War* (Princeton, N. J., 1957); David Riesman, *Thorstein Veblen: A Critical Interpretation* (New York, 1953).

11. Edmund S. Morgan, *The Puritan Dilemma: The Story of John Winthrop* (Boston, 1958); Broadus Mitchell, *Alexander Hamilton, Youth to Maturity, 1755–1788* (New York, 1957); Thomas P. Govan, *Nicholas Biddle, Nationalist and Public Banker* (Chicago, 1959); C. Vann Woodward, "George Fitzhugh, *Sui Generis*," in *Cannibals All!* by George Fitzhugh (Cambridge, Mass., 1960), vii–xxxix; Allan Nevins, *Study in Power: John D. Rockefeller* (2 vols., New York, 1953).

12. Richard Hofstadter, *The Age of Reform: From Bryan to F.D.R.* (New York, 1955); Marvin Meyers, *The Jacksonian Persuasion* (Stan-ford, Cal., 1957); Cecelia Kenyon, "Men of Little Faith: The Anti-Fed-eralists on the Nature of Representative Government," *William and Mary Quarterly*, XII (Jan., 1955), 3–43.

13. Hartz, *Liberal Tradition*.

14. For example: Will Herberg, *Protestant-Catholic-Jew: An Essay in American Religious Sociology* (New York, 1955); R. W. B. Lewis, *The American Adam: Innocence, Tragedy and Tradition in the Nine-teenth Century* (Chicago, 1955); Gabriel, *Course of American Demo-cratic Thought*. In sketching another version of the unity of American history, William B. Hesseltine adopted a quadruple rather than a triple calculus. See his presidential address, "Four American Traditions," *Journal of Southern History*, XXVII (Feb., 1961), 3–32.

15. Allan Nevins, *The War for the Union* (2 vols., New York, 1959– ), I, v; Rowland Berthoff, "The American Social Order: A Conserv-ative Hypothesis," *American Historical Review*, LXV (Apr., 1960), 495–514.

16. Boorstin, *The Americans,* 185–205.

17. Forrest McDonald, *We the People: The Economic Origins of the Constitution* (Chicago, 1958); Hammond, *Banks and Politics;* Robert P. Sharkey, *Money, Class and Party: An Economic Study of the Civil War and Reconstruction* (Baltimore, 1959); Robert H. Wiebe, "Business Disunity and the Progressive Movement, 1901–1914," *Mississippi Valley Historical Review,* XLIV (Mar., 1958), 664–85.

18. Charles V. Langlois and Charles Seignobos, *Introduction to the Study of History* (London, 1898), 279; Oscar Handlin et al., *Harvard Guide to American History* (Cambridge, Mass., 1954); Jacques Barzun and Henry Graff, *The Modern Researcher* (New York, 1958). One exception is Allan Nevins, *The Gateway to History* (Boston, 1938), 235– a book written with unprofessional gusto and addressed to a wide audience.

19. Isaiah Berlin, *Historical Inevitability* (London, 1954); Friedrich Meinecke, "Values and Causalities in History," *The Varieties of History,* ed. Fritz Stern (New York, 1956), 267–88; C. V. Wedgwood, *Truth and Opinion: Historical Essays* (London, 1960), 47–54; David Knowles, *The Historian and Character* (Cambridge, England, 1955); A. J. P. Taylor, *Rumours of Wars* (London, 1952), 9–13. The most cogent arguments on the other side of the issue—denying to the professional historian an ethical function—are also by Europeans: Herbert Butterfield, *History and Human Relations* (London, 1951), 101–30; Marc Bloch, *The Historian's Craft* (New York, 1953), 139–41; Geoffrey Barraclough, "History, Morals, and Politics," *International Affairs,* XXXIV (Jan., 1958), 1–15. A valuable essay by an American philosopher, defending the exercise of moral judgment by historians, came to my attention too late for use in this paper: Arthur Child, "Moral Judgment in History," *Ethics: An International Journal of Social, Political, and Legal Philosophy,* LXI (July, 1951), 297–308.

20. Charles W. Eliot, *Educational Reform: Essays and Addresses* (New York, 1909), 104–06.

21. Henry C. Lea, "Ethical Values in History," *Annual Report, American Historical Association, 1903* (2 vols., Washington, D.C., 1904), I, 53–69. This was the classic rebuttal, by an American scientific historian, to Lord Acton's famous protest in 1895 against the prevailing spirit of scientific neutrality: "I exhort you . . . to try others by the final maxim that governs your own lives, and to suffer no man and no cause to escape the undying penalty which history has the power to inflict on wrong." On this controversy, see Andrew Fish, "Acton, Creighton, and Lea: A Study in History and Ethics," *Pacific Historical Review,* XVI (Feb., 1947), 59–69, and John Emerich Edward Dalberg Acton, *Essays on Freedom and Power,* ed. Gertrude Himmelfarb (London, 1956), 41–52, 329–45.

22. Frederick Jackson Turner, "Social Forces in American History,"

in *The Frontier in American History* (New York, 1920), 323–32; James Harvey Robinson, *The New History: Essays Illustrating the Modern Historical Outlook* (New York, 1912).

23. For a parallel trend among philosophers, see Jay William Hudson, "Recent Shifts in Ethical Theory and Practice," *Philosophical Review*. XLIX (Mar., 1940), 105–20.

24. Although beset by such doubts in the 1930's, Beard fell back on an ultimate "act of faith" that history was moving "on an upward gradient toward a more ideal order." (Charles A. Beard, "Written History as an Act of Faith," *American Historical Review*, XXXIX [Jan., 1934], 226.)

25. Louis Gottschalk, *Understanding History* (New York, 1950), 10–13.

26. René Wellek, "Literary Scholarship," in *American Scholarship in the Twentieth Century*, ed. Merle Curti (Cambridge, Mass., 1953), 111–45.

27. For a balanced summary of these competing views of history, see W. H. Walsh, *An Introduction to Philosophy of History* (rev. ed., London, 1958).

28. Wilbur J. Cash, *The Mind of the South* (New York, 1941); Hannah Arendt, *The Human Condition* (Chicago, 1958); Lewis Mumford, *The City in History: Its Origins, Its Transformations, and Its Prospects* (New York, 1961). Two recent efforts by professional historians are C. Vann Woodward, *The Burden of Southern History* (Baton Rouge, La., 1960), and William R. Taylor, *Cavalier and Yankee: The Old South and American National Character* (New York, 1961).

29. Charles H. McIlwain, *The American Revolution: A Constitutional Interpretation* (New York, 1923), and Robert L. Schuyler, *Parliament and the British Empire* (New York, 1929); Herbert Butterfield, *George III and the Historians* (London, 1957). A reviewer of the last book observed: "It is perhaps the strangest thing of all to find so impressive a controversy reared on the insoluble, and to some extent uninteresting question of what exactly were the relationships between George III, the Duke of Newcastle, and the Earl of Bute in the years following 1760." (*Times Literary Supplement*, Nov. 22, 1957.)

30. For an unusual and pioneering inquiry of this kind, see Eric L. McKitrick, *Andrew Johnson and Reconstruction* (Chicago, 1960).

## CHAPTER 9

1. John Higham with Leonard Krieger and Felix Gilbert, *History* (New York, 1965), a volume in a series entitled *The Princeton Studies: Humanistic Scholarship in America* under the general editorship of Richard Schlatter. The final revisions in the manuscript were made in July, 1964.

2. John Higham, "The Cult of the 'American Consensus': Homogenizing Our History," *Commentary,* XXVII (Feb., 1959), 93–100.

3. Alfred D. Chandler, Jr., *Strategy and Structure: Chapters in the History of the Industrial Enterprise* (Cambridge, Mass., 1962); Stanley Elkins, *Slavery: A Problem in American Institutional and Intellectual Life* (Chicago, 1959); Eric McKitrick, *Andrew Johnson and Reconstruction* (Chicago, 1960); Richard McCormick, *The History of Voting in New Jersey* (New Brunswick, N.J., 1953), and "New Perspectives on Jacksonian Politics," *American Historical Review,* LXV (1960), 288–301. In American religious history the emergence of a new institutional approach may be observed in Sidney E. Mead's important article, "Denominationalism: The Shape of Protestantism in America," *Church History,* XXIII (Dec., 1954), 291–320.

4. Frank Thistlethwaite, *The Anglo-American Connection in the Early Nineteenth Century* (Philadelphia, 1959); David M. Potter, *People of Plenty: Economic Abundance and the American Character* (Chicago, 1954); Frank Tannenbaum, *Slave and Citizen: The Negro in the Americas* (New York, 1947).

5. Higham, *History,* 231–32. The importance we attached to a comparative approach shows especially in the contributions of my collaborators, Leonard Krieger and Felix Gilbert. The prospects for moral criticism are more fully developed in the preceding chapter.

6. Higham, *History,* 82–85, 132–44.

7. James Willard Hurst, *Law and Social Process in United States History* (Ann Arbor, Mich., 1960). See also Leonard W. Levy, *Legacy of Suppression: Freedom of Speech and Press in Early American History* (Cambridge, Mass., 1960), and George Lee Haskins, *Law and Authority in Early Massachusetts* (New York, 1960).

8. Robert H. Wiebe, *The Search for Order, 1877–1920* (New York, 1967).

9. David Fischer, *The Revolution of American Conservatism: The Federalist Party in the Era of Jeffersonian Democracy* (New York, 1965), 191. See also William N. Chambers, *Political Parties in a New Nation* (New York, 1963); Paul Goodman, *The Democratic-Republicans of Massachusetts: Politics in a Young Republic* (Cambridge, Mass., 1964); Richard P. McCormick, *The Second American Party System: Party Formation in the Jacksonian Era* (Chapel Hill, N.C., 1966); Joel Silbey, *The Shrine of Party: Congressional Voting Behavior, 1841–1852* (Pittsburgh, 1967); Lynn Marshall, "The Strange Still-Birth of the Whig Party," *American Historical Review,* LXXII (Jan., 1967), 445–68; W. R. Brock, *An American Crisis: Congress and Reconstruction, 1865–1867* (New York, 1963); J. Rogers Hollingsworth, *The Whirligig of Politics: The Democracy of Cleveland and Bryan* (Chicago, 1963); David J. Rothman, *Politics and Power: The United States Senate, 1869–1901* (Cambridge, Mass., 1966); Samuel P. Hays, "Social Analysis of

American Political History, 1880–1920," *Political Science Quarterly,* LXXX (Sept., 1965), 373–94. A shift of emphasis from section to party in interpreting American foreign policy is illustrated in Roger Brown's *The Republic in Peril: 1812* (New York, 1964).

10. (New York, 1966).

11. Daniel H. Calhoun, *Professional Lives in America: Structure and Aspiration, 1750–1850* (Cambridge, Mass., 1965); Roy Lubove, *The Professional Altruist: The Emergence of Social Work as a Career, 1880–1930* (Cambridge, Mass., 1965); Corinne Gilb, *Hidden Hierarchies: The Professions and Government* (New York, 1966).

12. Murray Murphey, "An Approach to the Historical Study of National Character," in *Context and Meaning in Cultural Anthropology,* ed. M. E. Spiro (New York, 1965), 144–63; Philip J. Greven, Jr., "Family Structure in Seventeenth-Century Andover, Massachusetts," *William and Mary Quarterly,* XXIII (Apr., 1966), 234–56. Another important contribution to the history of the American family is the account of inter-generational mobility in Stephan Thernstrom's *Poverty and Progress: Social Mobility in a Nineteenth Century City* (Cambridge, Mass., 1964).

13. Darrett B. Rutman, *Winthrop's Boston: Portrait of a Puritan Town, 1630–1649* (Chapel Hill, N.C., 1965); Roger Lane, *Policing the City: Boston, 1822–1885* (Cambridge, Mass., 1967); Sam Bass Warner, Jr., *The Private City: Philadelphia in Three Periods of Its Growth* (Philadelphia, 1968). See also Robert R. Dykstra, *The Cattle Towns* (New York, 1968), and Sumner Chilton Powell, *Puritan Village: The Formation of a New England Town* (Middletown, Conn., 1963).

14. The best account to date of what has been achieved through a quantitative approach to American political history is Allen G. Bogue's "United States: The 'New' Political History," *Journal of Contemporary History,* III (Jan., 1968), 5–27. On the parallel movement in economic history, see the judicious appraisal in the new introduction Stuart Bruchey has written for the paperback edition of his *The Roots of American Economic Growth, 1607–1861* (New York, 1968).

15. This division is strikingly revealed in Alfred H. Conrad, et al., "Slavery as an Obstacle to Economic Growth in the United States: A Panel Discussion," *Journal of Economic History,* XXVII (Dec., 1967), 518–60.

16. *Visible Saints: The History of a Puritan Idea* (New York, 1963); Gordon S. Wood, *The Creation of the American Republic, 1776–1787* (Chapel Hill, N.C., 1969). See also Laurence Veysey, *The Emergence of the American University* (Chicago, 1965); Morton and Lucia White, *The Intellectual Versus the City: From Thomas Jefferson to Frank Lloyd Wright* (Cambridge, Mass., 1962); and the important institutional interpretation advanced in George M. Fredrickson, *The Inner Civil War: Northern Intellectuals and the Crisis of the Union* (New York, 1965).

17. Louis Hartz et al., *The Founding of New Societies* (New York,

1964); Seymour Lipset, *The First New Nation: The United States in Historical and Comparative Perspective* (New York, 1963); J. R. Pole, *Political Representation in England and the Origins of the American Republic* (New York, 1966); Bernard Bailyn, *Education in the Forming of American Society* (Chapel Hill, N.C., 1960); Felix Gilbert, *To the Farewell Address: Ideas of Early American Foreign Policy* (Princeton, N.J., 1961); Eugene D. Genovese, *The Political Economy of Slavery: Studies in the Economy and Society of the Slave South* (New York, 1965); David Brion Davis, *The Problem of Slavery in Western Culture* (Ithaca, N.Y., 1966). See also *The Comparative Approach to American History,* ed. C. Vann Woodward (New York, 1968).

18. Marcus Hansen, *The Atlantic Migration, 1607–1860: A History of the Continuing Settlement of the United States* (Cambridge, Mass., 1940), and "Immigration as a Field for Historical Research," in *The Immigrant in American History* (Cambridge, Mass., 1940), 191–217; Richard Shryock, *The Development of Modern Medicine* (Philadelphia, 1936); Howard Mumford Jones, *America and French Culture, 1750–1848* (Chapel Hill, N.C., 1927); Merle Curti, *Probing Our Past* (New York, 1955), 191–286.

19. (2 vols., Princeton, N.J., 1959, 1964). For another major contribution by a historian of modern Europe, see Arno J. Mayer, *Politics and Diplomacy of Peacemaking: Containment and Counterrevolution at Versailles, 1918–1919* (New York, 1967).

20. Robert Kelley, *The Transatlantic Persuasion: The Liberal-Democratic Mind in the Age of Gladstone* (New York, 1969).

21. J. R. Pole, "The American Past: Is It Still Usable?" *Journal of American Studies,* 1 (Apr., 1967), 63.

22. Howard Zinn, "Abolitionists, Freedom-Riders, and the Tactics of Agitation," in *The Anti-Slavery Vanguard,* ed. Martin Duberman (Princeton, N.J., 1965), 417–51; Alan Heimert, *Religion and the American Mind: From the Great Awakening to the Revolution* (Cambridge, Mass., 1966). To date the important scholarship on these themes has come very largely from liberal rather than radical historians. Especially notable are: Winthrop D. Jordan, *White Over Black: American Attitudes Toward the Negro, 1550–1812* (Chapel Hill, 1968); August Meier, *Negro Thought in America, 1880–1915: Racial Ideologies in the Age of Booker T. Washington* (Ann Arbor, 1963).

23. See, for example, the fanfare accorded to *Towards a New Past: Dissenting Essays in American History,* ed. Barton J. Bernstein (New York, 1968), in the *American Historical Review,* LXXIV (Dec., 1968), 529–33, and in many other periodicals; and Irwin Unger's scrupulous examination of much minor writing, "The 'New Left' in American History: Some Recent Trends in United States Historiography," *American Historical Review,* LXXII (July, 1967), 1237–63.

24. In addition to Genovese's *Political Economy of Slavery,* see his "Rebelliousness and Docility in the Negro Slave: A Critique of the

Elkins Thesis," *Civil War History,* XIII (Dec., 1967) 293–314; also Gabriel Kolko, *The Triumph of Conservatism: a Reinterpretation of American History, 1900–1916* (New York, 1963), and "Brahmins and Business, 1870–1914: A Hypothesis on the Social Basis of Success in American History," in *The Critical Spirit: Essays in Honor of Herbert Marcuse,* ed. Kurt H. Wolff and Barrington Moore, Jr. (Boston, 1967), 343–63. Other important works in this vein are Michael Paul Rogin, *The Intellectuals and McCarthy: The Radical Specter* (Cambridge, Mass., 1967), and Michael B. Katz, *The Irony of Early School Reform: Educational Innovation in Mid-Nineteenth Century Massachusetts* (Cambridge, Mass., 1968).

25. Willie Lee Rose, *Rehearsal for Reconstruction: The Port Royal Experiment* (Indianapolis, 1964); Bernard Bailyn, *The Ideological Origins of the American Revolution* (Cambridge, Mass., 1967). See also Bailyn's *The Origins of American Politics* (New York, 1968).

26. Higham, *History,* 198–211, and Chapter 3 above.

27. Thomas S. Kuhn, *The Structure of Scientific Revolutions* (Chicago, 1962), 35–42.

# INDEX